Baby Blues® Scrapbook Number 8

One More and We're Outnumbered!

Rick Kirkman Jerry Scott

Baby Blues® Scrapbook Number 8

One More and We're Outnumbered!

by Rick Kirkman & Jerry Scott

Andrews and McMeel
A Universal Press Syndicate Company
Kansas City

 For information, write Andrews and McMeel, a Universal Press Syndicate Company, 4520 Main Street, Kansas City, Missouri 64111.

ISBN: 0-8362-2692-5

Library of Congress Catalog Card Number: 96-86650

To Abbey, who just keeps making life funner and funner.

—J.S.

To Drew and Jake, who already have their mom and dad outnumbered.

—R.K.

Other Baby Blues Scrapbooks from Andrews and McMeel

Guess Who Didn't Take a Nap?
I Thought Labor Ended When the Baby Was Born
We Are Experiencing Parental Difficulties . . . Please Stand By
Night of the Living Dad
I Saw Elvis in My Ultrasound

BABY BLUES®

RICK KIRKMAN / JERRY SCOTT

IT'S WEIRD HOW DIFFERENT HAM IS FROM ZOE AT THIS AGE...

SHE WAS COLICKY, AND HE'S PRETTY MELLOW MOST OF THE TIME... SHE BARELY SLEPT, AND HE SLEEPS SIXTEEN HOURS A DAY!

THEY'RE NOTHING ALIKE! NOTHING I LEARNED ABOUT RAISING A LITTLE GIRL APPLIES TO HIM! I HAVE TO START ALL OVER FROM SCRATCH!
KIRKMAN & SCOTT

TWO YEARS OF UNDER-GRADUATE MOTHERING, AND THIS KID CHANGES MY MAJOR!

HEY! WHAT'S HAM DOING IN BED WITH US?
Z

I PUT HIM HERE. IT'S A LOT EASIER TO HAVE HIM SLEEP WITH US WHILE I'M NURSING SO I DON'T HAVE TO KEEP GETTING UP IN THE MIDDLE OF THE NIGHT.
DO YOU THINK THAT'S OKAY?

WHAT IF IT WARPS HIS PERSONALITY? WHAT IF WE ACCIDENTLY ROLL OVER ON HIM IN OUR SLEEP.
WHAT IF I MADE **YOU** GET UP AND NURSE HIM EVERY TWO HOURS?

WELCOME ABOARD, LITTLE GUY!
KIRKMAN & SCOTT

I DON'T KNOW... IT JUST FEELS WEIRD TO HAVE THE BABY IN BED WITH US.
Z

WHY? PEOPLE HAVE BEEN SLEEPING WITH THEIR BABIES SINCE THE BEGINNING OF TIME! IT'S NATURAL! IT'S INSTINCTUAL!
BUT WHAT WOULD THE EXPERTS SAY?

EXPERTS? WHAT EXPERTS?? SPOCK? LEACH? BRAZELTON? HOW CAN THEY BE EXPERTS IN WHAT'S BEST FOR US? THEY DON'T EVEN KNOW US!

I WAS TALKING ABOUT OUR MOMS.
OH... **THOSE** EXPERTS.
KIRKMAN & SCOTT

GATE
32
MIAMI
IT'S REALLY GREAT TO HAVE YOU HERE, MOM... YOU, TOO, MOM.
THANKS, SWEETIE.
I CAN'T WAIT TO SEE THE NEW BABY!
KIRKMAN & SCOTT

MOST COUPLES WOULDN'T DREAM OF HAVING BOTH GRANDMAS COME TO HELP OUT WITH THE NEW BABY AT THE SAME TIME, BUT I THINK THIS WILL BE GREAT!
OF COURSE IT WILL BE, DEAR.
ABSOLUTELY, DARRYL.

AFTER ALL...THIS IS ABOUT COOPERATION, NOT COMPETITION.
SHOTGUN!
IN YOUR DREAMS, FOUR-EYES!

WE'RE HOME!
HI, GRANDMAS!

OOOH! THERE'S THAT BABY I'VE BEEN HEARING ABOUT!

AWWWWW!

HE LOOKS JUST LIKE YOUR FATHER!

AND WE THOUGHT THEY'D NEVER AGREE ON ANYTHING.
HE'S SO CUTE!
KITCHIE KITCHIE KOO!
KIRKMAN & SCOTT

I'M SO GLAD THEY DON'T HAVE A CAT.
ME TOO! YOU KNOW WHAT CATS CAN DO TO BABIES!

OH YES! THEY CAN SUCK THE BREATH RIGHT OUT OF THEM!
THAT'S RIGHT! THEY-
OH, COME ON! YOU DON'T REALLY BELIEVE THAT OLD WIVES' TALE, DO YOU?

NEVER USE THE TERM, "OLD WIVES' TALE" IN FRONT OF A COUPLE OF OLD WIVES.
KIRKMAN & SCOTT

BABY BLUES®
BY RICK KIRKMAN / JERRY SCOTT

I'M WEADY FOR MY CWOSEUP, MISTA DeMIW.

PSST! DARRYL! YOU HAVE TO COME AND SEE THE KIDS!

SHE'S "READING" TO HIM!
ISN'T THAT CUTE? GO GET THE VIDEO CAMERA.

NOW SHE'S SINGING HIM A SONG! HURRY UP!
OKAY! OKAY!

THIS IS SO ADORABLE! SHE JUST KISSED HIM!
THERE'S NO TAPE IN HERE!

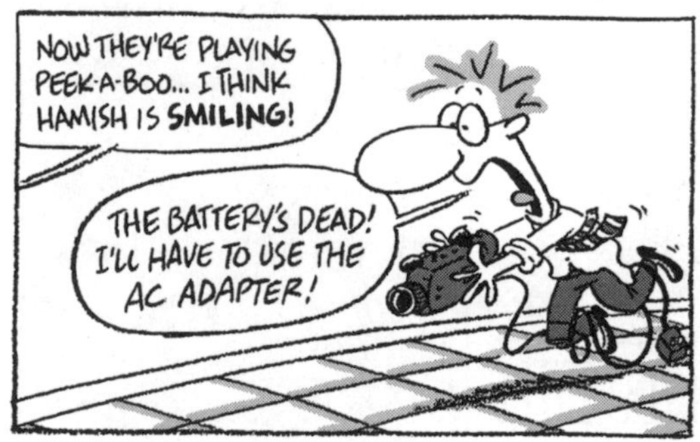
NOW THEY'RE PLAYING PEEK-A-BOO... I THINK HAMISH IS SMILING!
THE BATTERY'S DEAD! I'LL HAVE TO USE THE AC ADAPTER!

OKAY! I GOT IT! I'M READY! HERE WE GO!

WE-AAA-AAA-WE-AAA-AAA!
HE KICKED ME!
SIGH
KIRKMAN & SCOTT

SCREEECH!
SLAM!

WHAM!

SO THE MOTHERS-IN-LAW ARRIVED, HUH?
KISS! KISS! KISS! KISS! WOA, YEAH.
KIRKMAN & SCOTT

I HEARD YOUR MOM AND WANDA'S MOM ARE STAYING WITH YOU THIS WEEK.
THAT'S RIGHT. CAN YOU BELIEVE IT?

THEY BOTH INSISTED ON COMING TO HELP OUT WHILE WE GOT SETTLED WITH THE NEW BABY.
KIRKMAN & SCOTT

IT MUST BE NICE FOR WANDA TO HAVE ALL THAT HELP, BUT DON'T THEY ARGUE OVER WHO GETS TO HOLD THE BABY?
OH, NO... THEY WORKED OUT A SYSTEM.

ERF!
OOOF!
AAAGH!
UNGH!

SO HOW ARE YOU HOLDING UP WITH BOTH OUR MOMS HERE TO HELP OUT?
I DON'T KNOW...

THEY'VE TAKEN OVER EVERYTHING: THE CLEANING.., THE COOKING..., THE CHILD CARE...

I UNDERSTAND...
KIRKMAN & SCOTT

...YOU'RE READY FOR THEM TO GO HOME SO WE CAN GET OUR LIVES BACK TO NORMAL.
WHAT ARE YOU, NUTS?

SO THE MOTHERS-IN-LAW ARE STILL HERE?
YEAH... AND IT'S BEEN A LITTLE ROUGH.

EVERYTHING IS DIFFERENT WITH THEM AROUND. THE MEALS...THE KIDS' BEDTIME... THE DISCIPLINE...

NOTHING IS LIKE IT NORMALLY IS. IT REALLY GETS ON MY NERVES.
KIRKMAN & SCOTT

THEY'VE REALLY MESSED UP YOUR ROUTINE, HUH?
NO. THEY **IMPROVED** IT!

ISN'T THIS GREAT?
YEAH!

MY MOM IS READING TO ZOE, YOUR MOM IS ROCKING HAM TO SLEEP, THE HOUSE IS CLEAN, THE LAUNDRY IS DONE...
REALLY GREAT.

SINCE THEY GOT HERE EVERYTHING IS TOTALLY UNDER CONTROL!
YEP, REALLY, REALLY GREAT.

KIRKMAN & SCOTT

I WANT MY CHAOS BACK!

OKAY! THE CAR IS ALL LOADED! I GUESS WE'D BETTER GET GOING! WE DON'T WANT TO BE LATE!

GIVE GRANDMAS A KISS GOODBYE, ZOE! TELL THEM IT WAS GREAT HAVING THEM HERE!
KIRKMAN & SCOTT

I'LL BE WAITING OUT IN THE DRIVEWAY!

NINE HOURS TILL MY FLIGHT LEAVES... BETTER SAFE THAN SORRY.
WOULDN'T IT HAVE BEEN BETTER IF HE WAITED UNTIL I PACKED BEFORE PUTTING MY SUITCASE IN THE VAN?

BABY BLUES®
BY
RICK KIRKMAN / JERRY SCOTT

THE SITTER'S HERE!

HI, HONEY. WHERE'S ZOE?
SIGH! WATCHING TV.

I JUST NEEDED 30 MINUTES TO MYSELF, BUT I FEEL SO GUILTY!
WHY SHOULD YOU FEEL GUILTY FOR LETTING ZOE WATCH TV? IT'S A PROGRAM FOR KIDS, ISN'T IT?

YES, BUT SOME PEOPLE SAY THAT THE FAST-PACED, QUICK-EDIT TECHNIQUES THEY USE THESE DAYS CAN AFFECT ATTENTION SPANS.
SNAP! SNAP!
THAT'S RIDICULOUS...

...HOW COULD A SIMPLE KIDS PROGRAM LIKE THIS HAVE ANY EFFECT ON–

...YOUR ATTENTION SPAN?
WHAT ABOUT IT?
KIRKMAN & SCOTT

DO YOU HAVE TO GO POTTY, ZOE?
UH-HUH.

CODE YELLOW!

KIRKMAN & SCOTT

OH, WELL— WE'LL JUST HAVE TO START MOVING FASTER.
ARE YOU KIDDING? FIREFIGHTERS DON'T HAVE THIS KIND OF RESPONSE TIME!
UH-OH.

THUP! THUP! THUP!

LOOKS LIKE SOMEBODY NEEDS SOME ATTENTION.
THINK SO?
KIRKMAN & SCOTT

PWAY WIF BE-BE?
NO, ZOE. HE'S ASLEEP. YOU CAN'T PLAY WITH HIM UNTIL HE WAKES UP.
Z

Z

SPLISH!

WA-AA AA-AA!
HE WAKED UP!
KIRKMAN & SCOTT

I DON'T UNDERSTAND WHY HAM IS SO UPSET! I'VE BEEN PLAYING THE LULLABY TAPES FOR AN HOUR!

ZOE USED TO LOVE MUSIC, REMEMBER?
LET ME TRY.

HAM LIKES LULLABIES, TOO...HE JUST PREFERS HIS ELECTRIFIED.
RED HOT CHILI PEPPERS??
KIRKMAN & SCOTT

I WANT A DOULA.
WHAT'S A DOULA?

A DOULA IS A KIND OF SERVANT THAT SPECIALIZES IN HELPING NEW MOTHERS.

KIRKMAN & SCOTT

THEY DO ALL THE ENERGY-DRAINING HOUSEHOLD STUFF LIKE COOKING, CLEANING AND LAUNDRY SO MOMS CAN SPEND MORE TIME WITH THEIR BABIES.
WOW! THAT SOUNDS GREAT!

I WONDER IF THEY HAVE ANYTHING LIKE THAT FOR NEW DADS?
YEAH. THEY'RE CALLED WIVES.

WILL YOU HOLD HAM WHILE I TAKE A QUICK SHOWER?
SURE!

OW! OW! HEY! CUT THAT OUT!
KIRKMAN & SCOTT

OH. I FORGOT THAT HE MIGHT BE HUNGRY.
WHY DIDN'T YOU TELL ME TO PUT ON A SHIRT???

BABY BLUES®
BY
RICK KIRKMAN / JERRY SCOTT

DIVE! DIVE!

HEY LOOK! IT'S THE MacPHERSONS! AND THE NEW BAYYYBEEEEE!
OH NO!
NOT THE ARNETTES!

IS IT A BOY OR A GIRL?
BOY.
OOOOOOH! I JUST LOVE LITTLE BOYS!

HOW ABOUT THAT FACE?
OOOOOH! I JUST LOVE THAT FACE!

HOW ABOUT THAT HAIR?
OOOOOOH! I LOVE THAT HAIR!

WHAT'S HIS NAME?
HAMISH. HAM FOR SHORT.

UH...GOTTA GO.
BYE.

OOOOOH! I JUST LOVE THAT NAME!
IF I'D KNOWN IT WOULD'VE GOTTEN RID OF THE ARNETTES, I WOULD HAVE NAMED ZOE HAMISH, TOO!
KIRKMAN & SCOTT

OH LOOK! THAT NEW DISNEY MOVIE IS PLAYING AT THE MALL!
OH.

I COULD GET RHONDA TO STAY WITH HAMMIE, AND WE COULD TAKE ZOE THIS AFTERNOON! SHE'D LOVE IT!
YOU WANT TO GO SEE A MOVIE IN A THEATER FULL OF KIDS?

YEAH! I'M SO EXCITED, I CAN'T STAND IT!
MY THOUGHTS EXACTLY...
KIRKMAN & SCOTT

...EXCEPT FOR THE EXCITED PART.

YOU GUYS ARE REALLY GOING TO DO THIS, HUH?
I GUESS SO.
KNOCK IT OFF, DARRYL!

WE'RE TAKING ZOE TO HER FIRST DISNEY MOVIE... NOT CROSSING THE ALPS!

I SUGGEST YOU STOP THINKING OF THIS AS A CHORE, AND START TREATING IT AS AN OPPORTUNITY TO HAVE FUN!
OKAY.

KIRKMAN & SCOTT
WHEE.
HEY! WHO TOOK MY SUCKER?!

I'M GOING TO COMPLAIN.
IT'S NOT THAT BIG OF A DEAL.

BUT IT **BUGS** ME!
THIS IS A THEATER SHOWING A CHILDREN'S MOVIE! WHAT DO YOU EXPECT?

I DON'T CARE... I'M GOING TO FIND THE MANAGER.

YOUR FLOOR IS **WAY** TOO STICKY!
KIRKMAN & SCOTT

OKAY, HERE'S MOMMY'S POPCORN... HERE'S HER DRINK... HERE'S YOUR LICORICE... HERE'S YOUR DRINK... SOME EXTRA NAPKINS...
PSSST! SIT DOWN!
HEY-MISTER!

NOW THAT'S IT. THAT WAS THE LAST TIME I'M GETTING UP FOR ANYTHING.

NO MORE SNACKS, NO MORE FIDGETING... WE'RE ALL JUST GOING TO SIT HERE AND WATCH THE REST OF THE MOVIE TOGETHER. NO INTERRUPTIONS. NO EXCEPTIONS.
HAF'A POTTY.

KIRKMAN & SCOTT

THAT KID IS DRIVING ME NUTS WITH THAT STUPID CUP!
FWEEP! FWOOP! FWEEP! FWOOP!
DO YOU WANT ME TO TAKE IT AWAY FROM HIM?

DO YOU THINK HE'LL LET YOU?
FWEEP! FWOOP! FWEEP! FWOOP!
WE WON'T KNOW UNLESS I TRY.

HEY, KID, WE'RE TRYING TO WATCH THE MOVIE. GIVE ME THE CUP.
FWEEP! FWOOP! FWEEP!

KIRKMAN & SCOTT
DID HE GIVE IT TO YOU?
I'D RATHER NOT DISCUSS IT.

HI, GUYS! HOW WAS THE MOVIE?

GOOD!
ENLIGHTENING.
EDUCATIONAL.
YOU'RE KIDDING!

WHAT COULD YOU POSSIBLY LEARN FROM A CARTOON?
PLENTY.

FOR ONE THING, THAT THERE ARE KIDS WHO BEHAVE WORSE THAN OURS!
I DON'T KNOW WHETHER TO FEEL HAPPY FOR US, OR AFRAID FOR SOCIETY!
KIRKMAN & SCOTT

BABY BLUES®

BY RICK KIRKMAN / JERRY SCOTT

OKAY ⸗GASP!⸗...
THE BILLS ARE FINALLY PAID!

⸗GROAN!⸗ EIGHT LOADS OF LAUNDRY... WASHED, DRIED, FOLDED AND PUT AWAY!

KIRKMAN & SCOTT

I WISH YOU WOULDN'T MARTYR WHILE I'M MARTYRING.
HEY-I MARTYRED FIRST!

THE HOUSE IS A WRECK, THE SINK IS FULL OF DIRTY DISHES, THE KIDS CRIED ALL DAY, MY HAIR IS A MESS...

AND I THINK I'M THE LUCKIEST GUY IN THE WORLD!

REALLY?

BECAUSE YOUR FAMILY IS SO IMPORTANT TO YOU?
BECAUSE I COMMUTE.
KIRKMAN & SCOTT

SO HOW ARE YOU GUYS ADJUSTING TO THE NEW BABY?
PRETTY WELL, I THINK.

ALTHOUGH WE'VE BEEN HAVING SOME PROBLEMS WITH JEALOSY AND WHINING LATELY.

BUT THAT'S NOT TOO SURPRISING. THEY SAY THAT SOME REGRESSIVE BEHAVIOR IS NORMAL WHEN A NEW BABY IS BROUGHT INTO THE HOME...
KIRKMAN & SCOTT

I JUST SORT OF EXPECTED IT TO BE ZOE.
TUNA CASSEROLE AGAIN??

ZOE HOLD HAMMIE?
ZOE HOLD HAMMIE?
ZOE HOLD HAMMIE?
JUST A MINUTE, ZOE...

ZOE HOLD HAMMIE?
ZOE HOLD HAMMIE?
ZOE HOLD HAMMIE?
ZOE HOLD HAMMIE?
ZOE HOLD HAMMIE?
OKAY- YOU CAN HOLD HAMMIE WHILE I DECIDE WHAT TO MAKE FOR SUPPER.

KIRKMAN & SCOTT

I'M DONE!

HAM PWAY KETCH?
NO, ZOE,.. HAM IS JUST A TINY BABY.
THUP! THUP! THUP!

TINY BABIES ARE SO HELPLESS THAT THEY CAN'T EVEN HOLD THEIR HEADS UP.
OHHH.

KIRKMAN & SCOTT

LIKEWEN DADDY WATCH TV?
YES. LIKE WHEN DADDY WATCHES TV.
ZZ...

THEN:
JEEZ... HAVING A BABY IN THE HOUSE SURE CUTS DOWN ON THE TIME WE GET TO SPEND ALONE!
KIRKMAN & SCOTT

NOW:
HOW'S IT GOING?
DO I KNOW YOU?
WA-AA-AA

BABY BLUES®
BY
RICK KIRKMAN / JERRY SCOTT

Everything you always wanted to know about drain plugs*
*but were afraid to ask

BABY HAM IS LITTLE, SO WE GIVE HIM A BATH IN THE SINK- JUST LIKE WE USED TO WITH YOU!

WATZ DAT?

GULP! WELL, THERE IT IS. THE BIG QUESTION. THE ONE I'VE BEEN DREADING.
WATZ DAT?

IT'S OKAY... JUST RELAX. NO BIG DEAL.
WATZ DAT? WATZ DAT?

THE IMPORTANT THING IS TO RESPOND OPENLY AND HONESTLY WITHOUT ALARM...
WATZ DAT? WATZ DAT? WATZ DAT? WATZ DAT?
KIRKMAN & SCOTT

I DON'T KNOW! ASK YOUR FATHER!

IT'S THE DRAIN PLUG.
OH.

REMEMBER THIS MORNING WHEN I TOLD YOU ABOUT EVERYTHING I WANTED TO ACCOMPLISH TODAY?
YEAH...

I SAID I WANTED TO GET BOTH KIDS TO TAKE A NAP SO I COULD WEED THE FLOWER BED, FIX THE WALLPAPER IN THE BATHROOM AND MAKE A POT ROAST FOR DINNER, REMEMBER?
YEAH...

WELL, CONGRATULATE ME.
YOU ACTUALLY DID ALL THAT TODAY?

NO - I GOT BOTH KIDS TO TAKE A NAP... ONE MIRACLE AT A TIME!
KIRKMAN & SCOTT

DO YOU WANT TO HEAR SOMETHING WEIRD?

HAVING TWO KIDS ISN'T AS MUCH WORK AS I THOUGHT IT WOULD BE.

GET OUTTA HERE!
NO, REALLY! I EXPECTED THAT TWO KIDS WOULD BE TWICE AS MUCH CHAOS AND TWICE AS EXHAUSTING AS ONE, BUT IT'S NOT!
KIRKMAN & SCOTT

WELL THAT'S ENCOUR-AGING...
UNFORTUNATELY, IT'S **THREE** TIMES AS EXPENSIVE.

NOW THAT ZOE IS LEARNING TO USE THE POTTY ALL BY HERSELF, IT'S MADE THINGS A LOT EASIER FOR ME.

ALTHOUGH, WE SEEM TO BE GOING THROUGH A LOT MORE TOILET PAPER THAN WE USED TO...
KIRKMAN & SCOTT

MUNCH! MUNCH!
CHOMP! GNAW!
SLURP! CHOMP!

CLINK!
KIRKMAN & SCOTT

ARE YOU SURE YOU DON'T WANT TO SIT IN THE BOOSTER SEAT, ZOE?
NO.

BOY! IT'S WEIRD EATING WITHOUT THE KIDS AROUND... I SORT OF MISS THEM.

CHING! SPLASH!

SPLAT!

IS THAT BETTER?
KIRKMAN & SCOTT

HI DADDY.

IT'S TOO EARLY TO GET UP, ZOE. GO BACK TO BED FOR A WHILE.
OKAY.

DADDY I'M BACK.
TEN SECONDS IS NOT A "WHILE."

BABY BLUES®

BY RICK KIRKMAN / JERRY SCOTT

GEE, ZOE...YOUR SPEECH IS GETTING TO BE SO CLEAR AND UNDERSTANDABLE...
YOU SOUND LIKE SUCH A BIG GIRL!

IT'S REALLY NICE THAT YOU TAKE THE TIME TO COMPLIMENT HER LIKE THAT.

IT WASN'T A COMPLIMENT... IT WAS A COMPLAINT.
MORE MILK! HUWWY UP! WET'S GO!
KIRKMAN & SCOTT

I GUESS ZOE HAS REALLY OUTGROWN HER HIGH CHAIR.
LOOKS THAT WAY.

WE PROBABLY OUGHT TO FIX IT UP A LITTLE BEFORE HAM NEEDS IT.
FIX IT UP???
SCRITCH SCRITCH

YEAH. YOU KNOW...CLEAN IT UP. CHIP THE DRIED-ON FOOD OFF OF IT.
OH, THAT. WELL, OKAY...

BRRRA BBBB ABCK KKK
KIRKMAN & SCOTT

HI BUNNY.. WHAT'S WRONG?
MY NANNY QUIT!

HA! HA! HA! HA! HA! HA! HA! HA! HA! HA! HA!
KIRKMAN & SCOTT

YES! YES! YES! OH, YES!

GOSH, I'M SORRY TO HEAR THAT.

I'M SORRY TO HEAR YOUR NANNY QUIT, BUNNY. WHAT ARE YOU GOING TO DO?

SIGH! I DON'T KNOW.

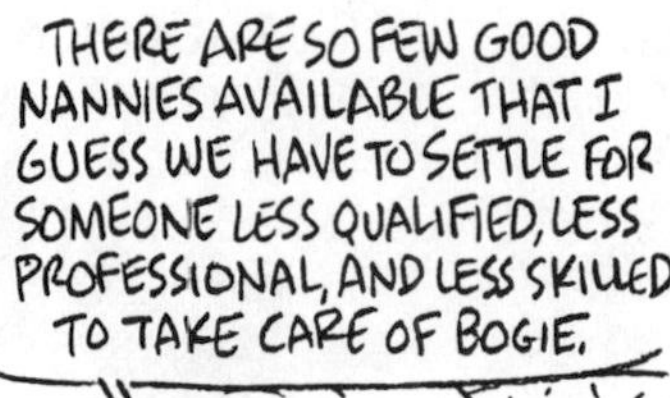
THERE ARE SO FEW GOOD NANNIES AVAILABLE THAT I GUESS WE HAVE TO SETTLE FOR SOMEONE LESS QUALIFIED, LESS PROFESSIONAL, AND LESS SKILLED TO TAKE CARE OF BOGIE.

KIRKMAN & SCOTT

SO ARE YOU INTERESTED IN THE JOB?
STOP. YOU'RE FLATTERING ME.

YOU'RE ASKING **ME** TO BE BOGIE'S NANNY?
IT WOULD JUST BE THREE DAYS A WEEK.

HUH-UH.
HE WOULDN'T BE ANY TROUBLE.
NO WAY.
HE AND ZOE WOULD ENTERTAIN EACH OTHER.
FORGET IT.
WE'LL PAY YOU SIX DOLLARS AN HOUR.

KIRKMAN & SCOTT

WANDA...?
JUST A SECOND– I'M REVERSING MY CONVICTIONS.

YOU'RE OFFERING ME SIX BUCKS AN HOUR FOR BABY-SITTING?
NOT BABY-SITTING... **CHILD CARING** IT'S THE GOING RATE.

THAT'S $144.00 A WEEK.
UH-HUH.
AROUND $575.00 A MONTH.
YEP.

I KNOW IT'S NOT MUCH, BUT THINK ABOUT IT AND LET ME...

...KNOW.
I'LL DO IT.
KIRKMAN & SCOTT

BABY BLUES®

BY RICK KIRKMAN / JERRY SCOTT

I GOT A JOB TODAY.
PBBBBTH!

WELL THANKS A LOT!
I'M SORRY... I DIDN'T MEAN TO BE SO SHOCKED THAT YOU GOT A JOB! YOU JUST SORT OF TOOK ME BY SURPRISE.

SO WHAT'S THE JOB?

I'M BUTCH AND BUNNY'S NEW NANNY.
PPBBBTH!
KIRKMAN & SCOTT

WHAT DO YOU MEAN YOU'RE BUTCH AND BUNNY'S NEW NANNY??
WELL, MAYBE "NANNY" ISN'T THE RIGHT WORD.

LET'S SAY THAT I'M LITTLE BOGART'S NEW CARE GIVER.
HIS CARE GIVER??

HIS SUPERVISOR? HIS STEWARD? HIS BABY SITTER?

MORE LIKE HIS "KEEPER."
HE'S NOT THAT BAD... BUNNY SAID HE'S STOPPED EATING FURNITURE.
KIRKMAN & SCOTT

YOU'RE ALREADY TAKING CARE OF ZOE AND HAM ALL DAY, WANDA. HOW ARE YOU GOING TO WATCH ANOTHER KID, TOO?

IT SHOULDN'T BE TOO BAD... BOGART'S A GOOD LITTLE BOY.
ARE YOU KIDDING?? HE'S A MONSTER!

HE'S A DESTRUCTIVE, ROWDY, NOISY, IRRITATING —
THEY'LL PAY ME $600 A MONTH.
KIRKMAN & SCOTT

—ADORABLE LITTLE MONSTER.
SEE? YOU'RE WARMING UP TO HIM ALREADY!

WE'RE HERE!
HI BOGART! COME ON IN!

NOW REMEMBER... NO HITTING, NO BITING, NO CLUBBING, NO POKING, NO PINCHING, NO SCRATCHING, NO ELBOWING, NO STOMPING, NO KICKING AND ESPECIALLY NO YOU-KNOW-WHAT!

DON'T WORRY- HE'LL BE FINE.

HE'LL BE FINE? WHAT ABOUT ME??
KIRKMAN & SCOTT

OKAY KIDS! IT'S OUR FIRST DAY TOGETHER... WHAT SHOULD WE DO?

COME ON! WHAT'LL IT BE? COLORING? LISTENING TO MUSIC? TAKING A WALK TO THE PARK?

WHATEVER IT IS, IT HAS TO BE SOMETHING THAT YOU CAN ALL DO TOGETHER.

SIGH!
KIRKMAN & SCOTT

BOGART! COME HERE.
BANG! BANG! BANG!

I DON'T THINK YOUR MOMMY AND DADDY WANT YOU TO BE PLAYING SUCH VIOLENT GAMES.

WHY DON'T YOU TRY PLAYING WITH SOMETHING A LITTLER GENTLER FOR A CHANGE.
K.

SIGH
BANG! BANG! BANG!
KIRKMAN & SCOTT

BABY BLUES®
BY
RICK KIRKMAN / JERRY SCOTT

IT'S SEVEN O'CLOCK, ZOE... TIME FOR YOUR BATH.
WHY?

OH NO YOU DON'T. I'M NOT FALLING FOR THAT AGAIN.

YOU ASK ME WHY AND I GIVE YOU A REASON. THEN YOU ASK ME WHY AND I GIVE YOU A REASON FOR THAT REASON... AND IT GOES ON AND ON.

WELL, IT'S NOT GOING TO WORK THIS TIME. I'M ON TO YOU.
WHY?

BECAUSE I'M YOUR FATHER.
WHY?

BECAUSE YOU'RE MY DAUGHTER.
WHY?
WHY?
WHY?
BECAUSE I'M MARRIED TO MOMMY.
WHY?
BECAUSE I LOVE HER.
WHY?
BECAUSE SHE'S A KIND, LOVING, GOOD PERSON.
WHY?
BECAUSE THAT'S HER NATURE.
WHY?
BECAUSE THAT'S THE WAY HER MIND WORKS.
BECAUSE HER BRAIN CHEMISTRY IS BALANCED.
BECAUSE THE N—

IT'S ALMOST 7:30... HAVEN'T YOU GIVEN HER A BATH YET?
KIRKMAN & SCOTT

ZOE! BOGART! QUIT FIGHTING!

BOGART! ZOE! STOP HITTING!

DON'T SCREAM! STOP PUSHING!
QUIT JUMPING!
RING! RING! RING!

HI, HONEY. HOW'S THE BABY SITTING JOB GOING?
I THINK I PULLED A MUSCLE IN MY JAW.
KIRKMAN & SCOTT

SORRY, HONEY... I DIDN'T MEAN TO BOTHER YOU WHILE YOU'RE BUSY.
THAT'S OKAY. I'M GLAD YOU CALLED.

WHY? DO YOU NEED SOMEONE TO TALK TO?
NOT REALLY...

... IT GIVES ME A CHANCE TO SEE IF IT'S STILL POSSIBLE FOR ME TO FORM A SENTENCE THAT DIDN'T START WITH "QUIT," "STOP," "DON'T" OR "LOOK OUT."
DONK!
KIRKMAN & SCOTT

THE BABY BLUES®
DAY CARE PRIMER

UNSUPERVISED CONFLICT RESOLUTION:
MINE!
MINE!

SUPERVISED CONFLICT RESOLUTION:
MINE!
MINE!
MINE!
KIRKMAN & SCOTT

HEY KIDS! DO YOU WANT TO GO TO THE PARK?
YES!
NO!

NO, BOGIE? WHY NOT? IT'LL BE FUN!

YOU AND ZOE CAN RIDE IN HER WAGON TOGETHER, AND YOU CAN RIDE ON THE SWINGS TOGETHER, YOU CAN SHARE ALL OF HER TOYS...
KIRKMAN & SCOTT

NOW DO YOU WANT TO GO?
YES!
NO!

WHAT WAS I THINKING WHEN I TOOK THIS JOB? WHAT MADE ME THINK THAT I COULD TAKE CARE OF MY OWN KIDS PLUS BE A NANNY TO THE KID NEXT DOOR?
THUP! THUP!

I'M JUST GOING TO HAVE TO TELL BUNNY THAT IT ISN'T WORKING. SHE'S REALLY GOING TO BE UPSET, BUT I CAN'T HELP IT. I'VE GOT TO BE STRONG.

BONK!

I'LL JUST SAY I'M SORRY, I QUIT. I'M SORRY, I RESIGN...
DING-DONG!

I'M SORRY...
YOU'RE FIRED.
KIRKMAN & SCOTT

BUNNY FIRED YOU?
YEAH, BUT I WAS GOING TO QUIT ANYWAY.

SHE FIRED ME BECAUSE SHE THOUGHT I WAS OVERWHELMED. BECAUSE SHE THOUGHT I COULDN'T HANDLE ANOTHER KID. BECAUSE SHE THOUGHT IT WOULD BE BEST FOR EVERY-BODY. SHOWS YOU WHAT SHE KNOWS!

WHY WERE YOU GOING TO QUIT?
BECAUSE I THOUGHT I WAS OVERWHELMED, BECAUSE I THOUGHT I COULDN'T HANDLE IT, AND BECAUSE I THOUGHT IT WAS THE BEST THING FOR EVERYBODY.

BIG DIFFERENCE.
YOU'RE TELLING ME!
KIRKMAN & SCOTT

BABY BLUES®

BY RICK KIRKMAN / JERRY SCOTT

LISTEN TO THIS...

BREAST MILK IS THE PERFECT FOOD FOR INFANTS. IN FACT, SCIENTISTS STILL HAVEN'T IDENTIFIED ALL THE NUTRITIONAL, HORMONAL AND GROWTH FACTORS IN HUMAN MILK.
KIRKMAN & SCOTT

I'M REALLY GLAD WE BREAST-FED BOTH OF OUR KIDS.

WE??

IT'S FUNNY...
...BEFORE I HAD KIDS I THOUGHT IT WOULD TAKE FOREVER TO GET BACK IN SHAPE AFTER PREGNANCY.
OF COURSE, NOW I KNOW THAT ISN'T TRUE...
...IT TAKES LONGER.
KIRKMAN & SCOTT

BOTTLE?
A BOTTLE? YOU DON'T USE A BOTTLE ANY MORE, ZOE!

BOTTLES ARE FOR BABIES, NOT FOR BIG GIRLS! YOU'RE A BIG GIRL, SO YOU DON'T NEED TO HAVE A BOTTLE ANY MORE, OKAY?

NUM-NUM?
KIRKMAN & SCOTT

HI, HONEY. HOW'S IT GOING TODAY?
OH FINE... HANG ON A MINUTE.

ZOE, DADDY IS ON THE PHONE! DO YOU WANT TO SAY HI TO DADDY?
NO.

SORRY.
NO? NO?? BUT I'M HER DADDY! HOW CAN SHE IGNORE ME WHEN I'M ON THE PHONE?
KIRKMAN & SCOTT

IF I WERE YOU, I'D EITHER GET USED TO IT OR RELEASE MYSELF ON VIDEO.

I CAN'T BELIEVE HOW FAT HAM IS GETTING!
NOT FAT... "HUSKY."

"HUSKY"?
YES, "FAT" HAS A NEGATIVE CONNOTATION, AND I DON'T WANT HAM TO THINK THAT WE'RE TALKING ABOUT HIM IN A NEGATIVE WAY.

IN FACT, I THINK WE SHOULD WATCH EVERYTHING WE SAY SO THE KIDS ARE NEVER EXPOSED TO NEGATIVE WORDS OR THOUGHTS AT HOME.
KIRKMAN & SCOTT

DO YOU THINK WE CAN DO THAT?
HUSKY CHANCE.

WOW! THAT'S SO TRUE.

WHAT?
THIS QUOTE: "IT TAKES A WHOLE VILLAGE TO RAISE A CHILD."

OH YEAH. I'VE HEARD THAT ONE BEFORE.
I WONDER WHO SAID THAT?
KIRKMAN & SCOTT

PROBABLY SOMEONE WHO TRIED IT BY THEMSELVES.

BABY BLUES®

BY RICK KIRKMAN / JERRY SCOTT

OH! A BABY PRESENT FOR HAM FROM COLLEEN AND MARTIN!
OPEN IT UP!

SIZE 0-3 MONTHS... PERFECT! HAM IS TWO MONTHS OLD TODAY.
OOH... PUT IT ON HIM.

UNH! UGH! OOOF!

I'LL NEVER UNDERSTAND BABY CLOTHES SIZES.
MAYBE IT'S A HAT.
KIRKMAN & SCOTT

IT'S BEEN SO LONG SINCE ZOE WAS TINY, I'D FORGOTTEN HOW GREAT IT FEELS TO CUDDLE A BABY.

THE FEEL OF THEIR SKIN... THE SMELL OF THEIR HEADS...

I'M HUNGWY!

...THE ABSENCE OF THEIR VOCABULARY...
KIRKMAN & SCOTT

SNIFF! SNIFF!

MMMM! RRROWW! KISS! KISS!
GIGGLE! GIGGLE!

SIGH!

I GUESS I'M ONE OF THOSE LUCKY WOMEN WHO FOUND A MAN WHO'S TURNED ON BY THE AROMA OF BABY BARF AND DESITIN.
KIRKMAN & SCOTT

ONE OF THE BEST THINGS ABOUT HAVING A TODDLER IS THAT IT'S EASY TO CHANGE THE SUBJECT.

WAIT... WHAT WERE WE JUST TALKING ABOUT?

BABY BLUES®

BY RICK KIRKMAN / JERRY SCOTT

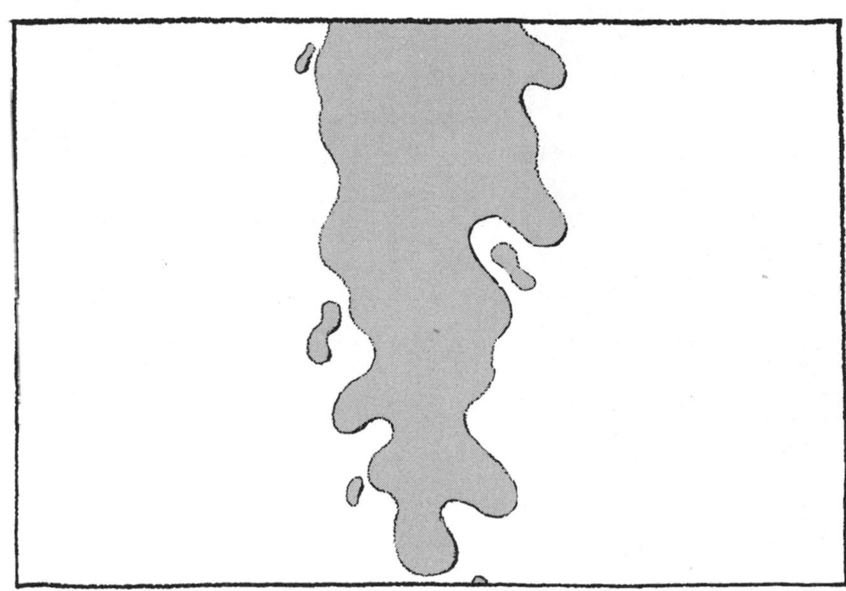

SHUT.

OPEN.

SHUT.

OPEN.
ZOE, DADDY IS TRYING TO TAKE A NAP.
WAS TRYING.
KIRKMAN & SCOTT

DID YOU KNOW THAT YOU'RE MY HERO?
I AM?

YOU'RE SO STRONG AND SMART AND BRAVE...
I GUESS I CAN HANDLE JUST ABOUT ANY SITUATION THAT COMES UP.

GOOD. WE'RE GOING OUT TO EAT TONIGHT, AND WE'RE TAKING THE KIDS.

YOU SET ME UP FOR THAT!
KIRKMAN & SCOTT

TABLE FOR FIVE, PLEASE.
FIVE? ARE YOU EXPECTING SOMEONE TO JOIN YOU LATER?

NO. JUST US...
KIRKMAN & SCOTT

...HER, ME, TWO KIDS AND THE DIAPER BAG.

YOU OUGHT TO SEE HIM, DAD.. HE'S REALLY GROWING FAST.

HE CAN HOLD HIS HEAD UP FOR A FEW SECONDS, HE CAN WAVE HIS ARMS—

YANK
BONK!
OW!

— AND HIS GRIP IS INCREDIBLE!
KIRKMAN & SCOTT

GASP! HAM JUST SMILED AT ME!
HE DID?

ARE YOU SURE? HE'S KIND OF YOUNG FOR THAT.
HE SMILED ALL RIGHT. IT WAS SUBTLE, BUT IT WAS DEFINITELY A SMILE.

SEE???
KIRKMAN & SCOTT

MAKE HIM DO IT AGAIN, I MUST HAVE BLINKED.
WHAT ARE YOU... BLIND?

I'M SO EXCITED THAT HAM SMILED AT ME YESTERDAY.
YOU SHOULD BE. IT'S A BIG DEAL.

I THINK BABIES REWARD PEOPLE THEY LOVE THE MOST WITH SMILES.

WELL, THAT MEANS HE OUGHT TO BE SMILING AT YOU PRETTY SOON THEN, TOO...
I CAN'T WAIT...

...SO FAR ALL I GET ARE THESE BLANK, DISBELIEVING STARES.
MAYBE YOU SHOULDN'T LET HIM SEE YOU UNTIL AFTER YOU SHOWER.
KIRKMAN & SCOTT

BABY BLUES®

RICK KIRKMAN / BY / JERRY SCOTT

LET'S PICK UP YOUR CRAYONS AND PUT THEM BACK IN THE BOX, OKAY, ZOE?

PICK UP THE CRAYONS.. PICK UP THE CRAYONS... SEE? JUST LIKE MOMMY IS DOING.
KIRKMAN & SCOTT

ONE AT A TIME. JUST LIKE THIS. HERE'S THE BLUE ONE... HERE'S A YELLOW ONE... A GREEN ONE... A BROWN ONE... AN ORANGE ONE... A PINK ONE... A PURPLE ONE...

SEE?
HEY, LOOK! ZOE PUT HER CRAYONS IN THE BOX ALL BY HERSELF!

NO, ZOE.

NO. DON'T COLOR ON THE WALL.

NO. DON'T THROW THAT!
NO. DON'T POUR THAT OUT.
NO. STAY OUT OF THERE.
NO. DON'T PICK THAT.

YOU OKAY, WANDA?
JUST CALL ME "MRS. NO-IT-ALL."
KIRKMAN & SCOTT

HAM HAS HIS FIRST DOCTOR'S APPOINTMENT TOMORROW.
OOOH... SHOTS.

NOW, WANDA, I DON'T WANT YOU TO BE NERVOUS. BE BOTH KNOW THAT THE RISK FOR SERIOUS REACTION TO IMMUNIZATION IS VERY SMALL, RIGHT?
RIGHT.
KIRKMAN & SCOTT

SO I DON'T WANT YOU TO GET ALL FREAKED OUT LIKE YOU DID WHEN ZOE GOT HER SHOTS.
I WON'T...

...BECAUSE YOU'RE TAKING HIM BY YOURSELF.
WHAT??

I'M GOING TO BE STRAIGHT WITH YOU, SON... WE'RE ON OUR WAY TO THE DOCTOR, AND YOU'RE GOING TO GET SOME SHOTS.

IT'S NOT GOING TO BE FUN, BUT THERE'S NOTHING TO BE AFRAID OF.

IT'S NO BIG DEAL, REALLY... JUST A LITTLE PAIN... NOTHING TO GET UPSET ABOUT...

HAMISH MacPHERSON?
HERE!
KIRKMAN & SCOTT

HEY, YOU'RE BACK! HOW DID IT GO?
GROAN! TERRIFIC.

TWO DIRTY DIAPERS, A THIRTY-MINUTE WAIT IN THE DOCTOR'S OFFICE, THREE SHOTS, A SCREAMING FIT YOU WOULDN'T BELIEVE, AND HE BARFED ON MY PANTS.

BOY, AM I GLAD THIS DAY IS OVER!
IT'S TEN-FIFTEEN IN THE MORNING.
KIRKMAN & SCOTT

DADDY...?
GOOD MORNING, SWEETHEART!

SAY... YOU LOOK LIKE YOU DON'T—

AHH-CHOOOPPPHT!

—FEEL TOO WELL.
GUESS WHO HAS A CASE OF THE SNIFFLES.
KIRKMAN & SCOTT

BABY BLUES®

RICK KIRKMAN / BY / JERRY SCOTT

DO YOU REMEMBER RON FROM ACCOUNTING?
YEAH. HIS WIFE'S NAME IS BARBARA AND THEY HAVE A TEENAGE SON, RIGHT?

RIGHT. WELL, GUESS WHAT? BARBARA IS PREGNANT.
YOU'RE KIDDING! SHE MUST BE IN HER FORTIES!

FORTY-THREE. RON SAYS THEY'RE REALLY EXCITED AND CAN'T WAIT TO EXPERIENCE THE JOYS OF PARENTHOOD ALL OVER AGAIN.

KIRKMAN & SCOTT

APPARENTLY THAT THEORY OF YOURS IS CORRECT.
PREGNANCY CAUSES AMNESIA.

ZOE, THAT'S HAM'S RATTLE. YOU CAN'T JUST TAKE IT AWAY FROM HIM LIKE THAT.
MINE!

IF YOU WANT THE RATTLE YOU HAVE TO GIVE HAM SOMETHING ELSE THAT'S FUN TO PLAY WITH, OKAY?
'K!

HERE!
KIRKMAN & SCOTT

MOMMY?
GO BACK TO SLEEP, ZOE.

DADDY?
GO BACK TO SLEEP, ZOE.

KIRKMAN & SCOTT

OPRAH?
I THOUGHT YOU WEREN'T LETTING HER WATCH DAYTIME TV ANYMORE!

HEY LOOK! ZOE'S DANCING!

THAT'S IT, ZOE! YOU'RE DOING GREAT!

WHEE! YEAH! YOU GO GIRL!
KIRKMAN & SCOTT

I WONDER IF SHE KNOWS HOW FUNNY SHE LOOKS...

TIME TO EAT, ZOE.
NO. MONKEY BAND.

YOU CAN WATCH THE "WHISTLING MONKEY COWBOY BAND" TAPE LATER... IT'S TIME TO EAT NOW.
NO! MONKEY BAND! MONKEY BAND!

EAT!
MONKEY BAND!
EAT!
MONKEY BAND!
KIRKMAN & SCOTT

WE'RE HAVING GUESTS FOR DINNER.
HOWDY! HOWDY! HOWDY!...

COOCHIE-COOCHIE-COO! COME ON HAMMIE- SMILE FOR DADDY!

COME ON... I KNOW YOU CAN DO IT! COME ON... ONE LITTLE SMILE...

SIGH
I DON'T GET IT...
KIRKMAN & SCOTT

...WHY WOULD A CUTE LITTLE KID LIKE YOU REFUSE TO SMILE AT HIS DADDY?
MAYBE HE GOT A PEEK AT THE BALANCE IN HIS COLLEGE FUND.

BABY BLUES®

BY RICK KIRKMAN / JERRY SCOTT

OKAY, DADDY NEEDS HIS SHOES NOW, ZOE.
NO. MINE.
CLOMP! CLOMP! CLOMP!

NO, THEY'RE DADDY'S SHOES, AND I NEED THEM SO I CAN GO TO WORK.
NO! MINE!

MINE!
MINE!!
MINE!
MINE!!!
KIRKMAN & SCOTT

CHILD DISCIPLINE BOOKS? THIRD SHELF ON YOUR LEFT.

SINCE WHEN CAN THEY SAY THAT ON TELEVISION??

THAT'S AWFUL! INEXCUSABLE! SHAMEFUL!
KIRKMAN & SCOTT

IF I WANTED TO HEAR THAT KIND OF LANGUAGE IN MY HOUSE, I'D DO MORE PLUMBING REPAIRS MYSELF!

WOOP!

WHOA!

HA! FINISHED!
KIRKMAN & SCOTT

I STILL DON'T ENJOY CHANGING DIAPERS, BUT SINCE HAM CAME ALONG MY REFLEXES HAVE REALLY IMPROVED!

EFK SQUMF SHON DOFFA... 'K?

OKAY.
KIRKMAN & SCOTT

NOW WE HAVE TO HOPE THAT WHATEVER IT IS WE JUST AGREED TO ISN'T SHARP, POISONOUS OR EXPENSIVE.

ZOE, WHY DON'T YOU SHARE ONE OF YOUR TOYS WITH HAM?
SHARWIF HAM?

SURE! WHY NOT? SHARING IS NICE. SHARING IS POLITE.

FUMP!
KIRKMAN & SCOTT

SHARWING IS FUN!

WHAT'S THE MATTER?
SOMETHING'S WRONG WITH THE VAN!
SLAM!

IT'S MAKING THIS LOUD "RATTLE CLANK SQUEAK KLONK!" SOUND EVERY TIME I GO AROUND A CORNER.
LET'S GO FOR A RIDE SO I CAN HEAR IT.

RATTLE CLANK SQUEAK KLONK!

I THINK I FOUND THE PROBLEM.
KIRKMAN & SCOTT

BABY BLUES®

BY RICK KIRKMAN / JERRY SCOTT

LIGHT.

WITE.
NO... LIGHT. L-L-L-L-L-IGHT.

LLLL...
YES! THAT'S IT! I THINK YOU'VE—

...WITE.
—GOT IT.
KIRKMAN & SCOTT

WHY? WHY? WHY? WHY? WHY? WHY? WHY? WHY? WHY? WHY? WHY? WHY? WHY? WHY? WHY?

BECAUSE. BECAUSE. BECAUSE. BECAUSE. BECAUSE. BECAUSE. BECAUSE. BECAUSE. BECAUSE. BECAUSE. BECAUSE. BECAUSE. BECAUSE. BECAUSE. BECAUSE.

OH, O'TAY.
KIRKMAN & SCOTT

SEE? ALL SHE WANTS IS SOLID REASONING.
I GIVE UP.

HERE... LET ME WATCH THE KIDS FOR A WHILE.
REALLY?

THAT'S SWEET OF YOU.
MY PLEASURE.

THERE'S NOTHING MORE IMPORTANT A FATHER CAN DO THAN SPEND TIME ALONE WITH HIS CHILDREN IN THE EVENING.

PLUS, IT GETS HIM OUT OF DOING THE DISHES.
KIRKMAN & SCOTT

WAA-AAA-AAA-AAA
IT'S NO USE! I'VE TRIED EVERYTHING, AND HE STILL WON'T STOP CRYING!

WAA-AAA-AAA-AAA
I DON'T UNDERSTAND IT! NOTHING THAT WORKED WITH ZOE WORKS WITH HAM...
IT'S NOT FAIR!
KIRKMAN & SCOTT

WAA-AAA-AAA-AAA
THERE OUGHT TO BE A RULE THAT SAYS IF YOUR FIRST CHILD IS DIFFICULT, THE NEXT ONE IS AUTOMATICALLY EASIER.
YEAH... WE CAN PUT IT RIGHT AFTER THE RULE THAT SAYS LABOR PAINS EARN YOU FREQUENT FLIER MILES.

DADDY!
ZOE?

MOMMY! DADDY! MOMMY! DADDY!
WE'RE COMING, ZOE! WE'RE COMING!
KIRKMAN & SCOTT

WE'RE HERE, ZOE!! WHAT'S WRONG?

SEE? BEWWY BUTTON!
OH...
THANK GOODNESS WE MADE IT IN TIME.

IT SEEMS LIKE I'M NOT READING AS MUCH OF THE PAPER AS I USED TO.

SINCE THE KIDS CAME ALONG, I'M TOO BUSY TO KEEP UP WITH POLITICS, I DON'T HAVE TIME TO READ ABOUT SPORTS, AND I'M JUST TOO TIRED TO LOOK AT THE BUSINESS SECTION.
Life

SIGH! THE ONLY SECTIONS I REALLY RELATE TO ARE THE OBITUARIES AND THE COMICS.
KIRKMAN & SCOTT

BABY BLUES®
BY
RICK KIRKMAN / JERRY SCOTT

SO, WHAT DO YOU THINK?
WHAT DO I THINK ABOUT WHAT?

ANYTHING! EVERYTHING! POLITICS... SPORTS... REAL ESTATE... I DON'T CARE!

I'VE BEEN COOPED UP IN THIS HOUSE ALL DAY FEEDING THE KIDS, ENTERTAINING THE KIDS, AND CLEANING UP AFTER THE KIDS, SO I JUST WANT TO TALK ABOUT SOMETHING BESIDES THE KIDS!
OKAY. I'M SORRY... WHY DIDN'T YOU SAY SO?

SO—WHAT'S ON YOUR MIND?
THE KIDS.

HAVE YOU NOTICED THAT WE ONLY HAVE ONE THING IN COMMON ANYMORE?

HUH?
THINK ABOUT IT... WE DON'T GO OUT TO EAT ALL THE TIME LIKE WE USED TO, WE DON'T GO TO THE MOVIES, AND WE DON'T SKI, BIKE OR HIKE ANYMORE.

PRACTICALLY ALL OF OUR ENERGY IS SPENT ON THIS ONE SINGLE, NARROW, SPECIFIC EFFORT.

TRYING TO STAY AWAKE PAST TEN O'CLOCK?
NO! RAISING THE KIDS!
KIRKMAN & SCOTT

Z
Z...!
KIRKMAN & SCOTT

OHMY GOSH!

WHAT'S WRONG?
I HAD A NIGHTMARE WHERE YOU WERE THE VICTIM OF A NEARLY UNSOLVABLE MURDER, AND I WAS SUDDENLY FACED WITH SPENDING THE REST OF MY LIFE CAVORTING ON THE BEACH WITH A BUNCH OF LONG-LEGGED BLONDES IN BIKINIS!

I MUST BE WATCHING TOO MANY DETECTIVE SHOWS.
SPONSORED BY WAY TOO MANY BEER COMMERCIALS.

MAAA-MAAAAA MAAA-MAAAA AAAAA!

MAAAA-MAAAA NO! MINE! MAAAA MAAAAA MOMMEEEE! MINE! NO!

MOMMEEEE! GIMMEE MAMA MAA-MINE MAAA MAAAA I WANNA MAAA-MAAA! GIMMEE MOMMY! I WANNA!
KIRKMAN & SCOTT

ANOTHER ONE OF THOSE DAYS, HUH?
TELL ME AGAIN HOW LONG THE "TERRIBLE TWO'S" ARE SUPPOSED TO LAST.

I REALLY LIKE HAVING CHILDREN.

I LIKE THE SOUNDS, I LIKE THE ACTIVITY, I LIKE THE HUMOR...
KIRKMAN & SCOTT

DON'T JUST STAND THERE! WE HAVE A STUFFED WALRUS STUCK IN THE TOILET AND IT'S FLOODING THE WHOLE BATHROOM!

...**ESPECIALLY** THE HUMOR.
SPLUSH THUP! SPLUSH THUP!

DARRYL, COME AND SEE ZOE.

JUST LOOK AT HER... NO INHIBITIONS... NO WORRIES. JUST THE PURE JOY OF PLAYING NAKED IN THE RAIN.
HEE HEE HEE HEE!

IT SORT OF MAKES YOU THINK, DOESN'T IT?
YEAH.

WE OUGHT TO BE MORE SPONTANEOUS.
IT'S RAINING! I DON'T HAVE TO MOW!
KIRKMAN & SCOTT

HA! HA! HA!
WHAT'S SO FUNNY?
PHOTOS

YOU MUST HAVE TAKEN THESE BACK WHEN ZOE WAS JUST A BABY. GET A LOAD OF THOSE SLOPPY CLOTHES! AND THAT HAIR! WHOA! WAS I REALLY THAT FAT?

THAT'S THE ROLL OF FILM WE TOOK LAST WEEKEND.
PHOTOS
KIRKMAN & SCOTT

IF IT'S ANY CONSOLATION, I THINK YOUR HAIR LOOKS NICE TODAY.
IF ANYBODY NEEDS ME I'LL BE IN THE COOKIE JAR.

BABY BLUES®

BY RICK KIRKMAN / JERRY SCOTT

DA-DEE!

I LOVE THIS.

GETTING THIS KIND OF GREETING AFTER A HARD DAY'S WORK REMINDS ME THAT I'M MORE THAN JUST A PAYCHECK...
KIRKMAN & SCOTT

... I'M ALSO A NAPKIN.

THESE REMOTES ARE AMAZING.

WITH JUST THE PUSH OF A BUTTON THE REMOTE CONTROL BRINGS A NEW LEVEL OF EFFICIENCY AND ENJOYMENT TO MILLIONS OF PEOPLE.
KIRKMAN & SCOTT

AIEEAIEEEAIEEE!
CLACK!
CLAK!

NOW IF THEY JUST MADE ONE OF THESE THAT WORKED ON KIDS...
BUT IT WOULD ONLY NEED TWO BUTTONS- "VOLUME DOWN" AND "PAUSE."

DO YOU EVER FIND YOURSELF SILENTLY CRITICIZING THE WAY OTHER PEOPLE RAISE THEIR KIDS?

HEY, LADY! IF I SEE YOU YANK ON YOUR LITTLE BOY'S ARM LIKE THAT AGAIN, I'M GOING TO TEAR YOU TO PIECES!!
KIRKMAN & SCOTT

WHAT DO YOU MEAN BY "SILENTLY"?

HOW'S MY FAVORITE NEPHEW?
OH! SINCE YOU'RE HERE, I'LL GIVE YOU YOUR BABY ANNOUNCEMENT SO I WON'T HAVE TO MAIL IT.

AWW... HOW CUTE! THESE ARE GREAT!
FOR THE PAST COUPLE OF WEEKS I'VE DEVOTED EVERY SPARE SECOND TO WRITING AND ADDRESSING THESE THINGS...

A PICTURE... A PERSONAL NOTE... A LITTLE BLUE RIBBON... YOU'RE INCREDIBLE!
THANK YOU.

SO HOW MANY OF THESE DO YOU HAVE FINISHED?
COUNTING YOURS... ONE.
KIRKMAN & SCOTT

WANDA, HAVE YOU SEEN MY SNEAKERS?
SO, ANYWAY, MOM CALLS AND SAYS–
MAMA LOOK... KITTY GO BYE-BYE?

...THAT SHE WANTS–
–VERY NICE SWEETIE–
–THEY'RE IN THE GARAGE–
–TO GO ON A CRUISE! CAN YOU BELIEVE THAT?

WAIT! I CAN'T CONCENTRATE IF THERE'S MORE THAN ONE CONVERSATION GOING ON AT A TIME!
REALLY? I CAN'T CONCENTRATE IF THERE **ISN'T!**
KIRKMAN & SCOTT

REMEMBER WHEN WE WOULD TRY TO GET READY TO GO VISIT SOMEONE WHEN ZOE WAS A BABY?
YEP.

I THINK OUR RECORD TIME FOR GETTING OUT OF THE HOUSE WAS TWO HOURS AND SIXTEEN MINUTES.
YEAH! CAN YOU BELIEVE THAT?

KIRKMAN & SCOTT

HOW DID WE EVER DO IT SO **FAST?**
BEATS ME.

I REMEMER ALWAYS WISHING FOR A LITTLE BROTHER OR SISTER.

DOES KEESHA ALWAYS WHINE LIKE THAT?

NO... DOES ZOE ALWAYS HIT OTHER CHILDREN WHEN SHE DOESN'T GET HER WAY?
BONK!
NO.

DO YOU ALWAYS CRITICIZE OTHER PEOPLE'S CHILDREN?

KIRKMAN & SCOTT
YES.

I JUST RAN ACROSS ZOE'S BABY BOOK.

THE FIRST FEW MONTHS ARE REALLY CRAMMED WITH PICTURES, NOTES, MEMENTOS AND CLIPPINGS, BUT TOWARD THE END THERE'S A LOT LESS STUFF.

YEAH, YOU'RE RIGHT. I GUESS WE GOT TOO BUSY TO KEEP IT UP.

I WONDER IF HAM'S BABY BOOK WILL BE LIKE THAT?
I GUESS IT DEPENDS ON WHETHER OR NOT WE EVER TAKE IT OUT OF THE WRAPPER.
BABY
KIRKMAN & SCOTT

WHEN WE PUT ZOE DOWN FOR A NAP AT THIS AGE WE SPENT THE WHOLE TIME WORRYING ABOUT HER.
I REMEMBER.

WAS SHE WARM ENOUGH? WAS SHE TOO WARM? SHOULD SHE LIE ON HER BACK OR ON HER STOMACH? SHOULD WE PLAY SOFT MUSIC? SHOULD WE LEAVE THE DOOR OPEN OR SHUT?

WITH HAMMIE, WE JUST PLOP HIM DOWN IN THE CRIB AND THAT'S THAT!
KIRKMAN & SCOTT

HAVE WE GOTTEN SMART OR HAVE WE GOTTEN COMPLACENT?
WE'VE GOTTEN TIRED.

COME ON, ZOE!
OPEN YOUR MOUTH!

DON'T... HEY!
QUIT IT... STOP... JUST LET ME...
UNH! UNH!

OKAY! I GIVE UP!

SO SOON??
KIRKMAN & SCOTT

!

LOOK AT ME!
WHAT?

I'M WEARING SENSIBLE "DAD PANTS" WITH AN ELASTIC WAIST-BAND, MY POCKETS ARE FULL OF KLEENEX, RAISINS AND CHEERIOS, MY SHIRT HAS A BIG DROOL STAIN, AND THERE'S A "BARNEY" STICKER ON MY BUTT.

AM I GOING TO LOOK THIS "DADDY-ISH" FOR THE REST OF MY LIFE?
ONCE A PARENT, ALWAYS APPARENT.
KIRKMAN & SCOTT

DO YOU HAVE TO GO POTTY, ZOE?
NO.

DO YOU HAVE TO GO POTTY NOW, ZOE?
NO.

DO YOU HAVE TO GO POTTY NOW, ZOE?
NO.
KIRKMAN & SCOTT

HAFTA GO POTTY NOW.

BABY BLUES®

BY RICK KIRKMAN / JERRY SCOTT

OHMYGOD!
OHMYGOD!
OHMY GOD!

OHMYGOD!
OHMYGOD!
OHMYGOD!
WANDA! STOP SAYING "OH MY GOD!" AND TELL ME WHAT'S WRONG!

MY DAD HAD A HEART ATTACK! I'LL HAVE TO GO THERE. I'LL TAKE HAMMIE WITH ME. I'D BETTER CALL THE AIRLINE RIGHT AWAY.
KIRKMAN & SCOTT

THAT MEANS YOU'LL HAVE TO TAKE CARE OF ZOE ALL BY YOURSELF FOR A FEW DAYS.
OHMYGOD!
OHMYGOD!
OHMYGOD!

THE DOCTORS SAID THAT IT WAS A MILD HEART ATTACK, AND THAT DAD WILL PROBABLY BE OKAY.
THAT'S GOOD.

YEAH. HE'S OUT OF INTENSIVE CARE ALREADY AND FEELING MUCH BETTER.
IF HE'S DOING SO WELL, MAYBE YOU DON'T HAVE TO GO RIGHT AWAY.

I'M NOT GOING JUST FOR HIM. I'M GOING FOR MOM AND FOR RHONDA AND ME, TOO.

A HEART ATTACK DOESN'T ATTACK JUST ONE HEART.
KIRKMAN & SCOTT

OKAY. MY BOSS SAID I CAN USE A FEW VACATION DAYS TO STAY HOME WITH ZOE WHILE YOU'RE GONE.
GREAT! THANKS, HONEY.

NO PROBLEM. YOU JUST GO SEE YOUR DAD. THAT'S ALL THAT COUNTS. DON'T WORRY ABOUT US. ZOE AND I WILL BE FINE HERE ALL BY OURSELVES. JUST FINE. REALLY. YEP. UH-HUH.

WHO ARE YOU TRYING TO CONVINCE... ME OR YOU?
BOTH OF US.
KIRKMAN & SCOTT

ZOE, GRANDPAPPY GOT SICK, SO MOMMY IS GOING TO HELP HIM GET BETTER, OKAY?
K.

AND I'M TAKING HAMMIE WITH ME BECAUSE HE'S JUST A LITTLE BABY, OKAY?
K.

AND YOU GET TO STAY HERE WITH DADDY, OKAY?

PIZZA?
EVERY NIGHT.
K.
WHAT DID SHE SAY?
NEVER MIND.
KIRKMAN & SCOTT

I GUESS THAT'S EVERYTHING... HAVE A GOOD FLIGHT.
I WILL.

TELL YOUR DAD I'M THINKING OF HIM AND I HOPE HE GETS WELL SOON!

GATE 22

GATE 21

WAAAAAAA!
REEEALLY SOON.
KIRKMAN & SCOTT

WHEW! I FORGOT HOW HARD IT IS TO FLY WITH A BABY!

THIS IS RIDICULOUS! THERE'S JUST TOO MUCH TO DEAL WITH!

THE DIAPER BAG, THE CAR SEAT, THE CARRY-ON BAG...
KIRKMAN & SCOTT

...NOT TO MENTION THE CROWD REACTION.
NOT HERE!
OH NO!
NUTS!
WHY ME??

BABY BLUES®
BY
RICK KIRKMAN / JERRY SCOTT

THE BABY SITTER IS HERE.
GREAT. I'M ALMOST READY.

YOU KNOW, I'M REALLY LOOKING FORWARD TO GOING OUT BY OURSELVES, BUT I'M SORT OF DREADING IT, TOO.
I KNOW WHAT YOU MEAN.

IT BREAKS MY HEART TO SEE THE KIDS CARRYING ON WHENEVER WE GO ANYPLACE WITHOUT THEM.
THE CRYING, THE SCREAMING, THE CLINGING... IT'S ALMOST UNBEARABLE!

:SIGH: WELL, HERE GOES NOTHING...
OKAY... MOMMY AND DADDY ARE LEAVING NOW. WE'LL BE BACK LATER!

'K. BYE.

KIRKMAN & SCOTT

WELL, HAMMIE, IT LOOKS LIKE JUST YOU AND ME FOR THE NEXT FEW DAYS.

BUT DON'T WORRY... WE'LL FIND LOTS TO DO! WE'LL VISIT GRAND-PA IN THE HOSPITAL, WE'LL FEED THE DUCKS AT THE PARK, WE'LL TAKE GRANDMA SHOPPING...

WHY, I'LL BET WE END UP DOING ALMOST AS MANY FUN AND CREATIVE THINGS AS DADDY AND ZOE ARE GOING TO DO!

WHERE'S THE REST OF YOUR CHILDREN'S VIDEO SECTION?
YOU'R HOLDING IT.
NEW RELEA
REWIND OR ELSE!
KIRKMAN & SCOTT

LADY! WHAT ARE YOU DOING??

FEEDING MY BABY.
RIGHT HERE? ON AN AIRPLANE?? IN FRONT OF EVERYBODY??

LOOK, IF IT MAKES YOU UNCOMFORTABLE, I'LL JUST GO SOMEWHERE ELSE.
YES. PLEASE. THANK YOU.

DISGUSTING!
PLAYBABE
KIRKMAN & SCOTT

UH-OH... I THINK MOMMY NEEDS TO CHANGE YOUR PANTS.

LET'S SEE... WE'LL NEED A DIAPER, THE WIPES, SOME DESITIN...
KIRKMAN & SCOTT

...AND A **REALLY** GOOD SENSE OF HUMOR.
CHANGING TABLE

HERE'S YOUR TOMATO JUICE.
THANKS.

WHAP!
KIRKMAN & SCOTT

COULD YOU GET ME SOMETHING?
YES, MA'AM. YOU BET. OUR AIRLINE PRIDES ITSELF ON SERVICE. THE CUSTOMER'S NEEDS ALWAYS COME FIRST!

HERE, TAKE AS MANY AS YOU WANT.
NUTS
NUTS
NUTS

MOMMY! MOMMMMY! MOMMY!
MOMMY WILL BE BACK IN A COUPLE OF DAYS, ZOE... NOW GO BACK TO SLEEP.

SWEEP WIF YOU!
WHAT? WELL, ALL RIGHT... I GUESS IT'LL BE OKAY.

BUT REMEMBER- NO SQUIRMING, NO KICKING, NO FIDGETING...

...AND NO HOGGING THE BED.
Z
KIRKMAN & SCOTT

PUNCH! PUNCH!

PUNCH!
WAP!
WAP!
SOCK!

WAPPITY! WAPPITY! WAPPITY!
BOOF!
POW

I DON'T CARE IF YOU ARE SCARED... TOMORROW NIGHT YOU'RE SLEEPING IN YOUR OWN BED.
Z
DONK!
KIRKMAN & SCOTT

BABY BLUES®

BY RICK KIRKMAN / JERRY SCOTT

I'M SO GLAD YOU'RE GOING TO BE OKAY, DADDY!
KIRKMAN & SCOTT

I STILL CAN'T BELIEVE YOU HAD A HEART ATTACK. IT JUST DOESN'T SEEM REAL... I MEAN, HEART ATTACKS ARE FOR OLD PEOPLE!

I'M TOO YOUNG FOR YOU TO BE OLD!
THAT'S FUNNY... YOUR MOTHER SAID THE SAME THING.

WELL, ZOE, IT'S BEEN A ROUGH MORNING, BUT WE DID IT.

WE GOT BREAKFAST, YOUR FACE WASHED, YOUR TEETH BRUSHED, YOUR HAIR COMBED, YOUR CLOTHES ON, AND IT'S ONLY...

...FOUR P.M.
KIRKMAN & SCOTT

HI HONEY. IT'S ME. I'M JUST CALLING TO SEE HOW YOU'RE DOING.

WE'RE FINE! JUST FINE!

HOW'S THE HOUSE?
THE HOUSE? THE HOUSE IS FINE! WHY WOULDN'T IT BE FINE? EVERYTHING IS UNDER CONTROL! NO PROBLEMS!

SHE KNOWS!!

HEE! HEE! ISN'T THAT CUTE? I SHOULD GET THE CAMERA.

I'VE NEVER SEEN HER THIS INVOLVED IN ANYTHING. WHATEVER IT IS SHE'S PLAYING WITH HAS HER TOTALLY FASCINATED LIKE NOTHING EVER HAS BEF—

MY WALLET!!
KIRKMAN & SCOTT

MOMMY IS COMING HOME TODAY! HEY! MOMMY IS COMING HOME!
SNAP! SNAP!

NOW DADDY WON'T HAVE TO COOK AND CLEAN... NO LAUNDRY AND SHOPPING TOO!
ARRIVALS
DEPARTURES

'CAUSE MOMMY IS COMING HO-O-O-O-O-OME!
GATE 1
KIRKMAN & SCOTT

ZOE REALLY MISSED YOU.

WAA-AA-AA-AA-AA!
UH-OH... ZOE'S CRYING.
THAT'S NOT ZOE, IT'S HAM!

WAA-AA-AA-AA-AA!
IT IS?
YES! CAN'T YOU TELL THE DIFFERENCE?

WELL, OF COURSE I... SURE I... WHAT KIND OF QUEST—

WAA-AA-AA-AA-A!
-I GUESS I CAN'T.
THEN YOU NEED MORE PRACTICE.
KIRKMAN & SCOTT

BABY BLUES®
BY
RICK KIRKMAN / JERRY SCOTT

DIVE! DIVE!

AHHHHH...

I LOVE MY FAMILY, BUT IT REALLY FEELS GOOD TO BE ALONE FOR A WHILE.

NO DIAPERS... NO FEEDINGS... NO TELEPHONES... NO QUESTIONS...

...JUST THIRTY GLORIOUS MINUTES OF UNINTERRUPTED BLISS IN A WARM BUBBLE BATH.

JUST SO YOU ALL KNOW, I'M HAVING A WONDERFUL TIME AND I'M REALLY GRATEFUL FOR THIS OPPORTUNITY.
KIRKMAN & SCOTT

OF COURSE, SOME OPPORTUNITIES ARE GIVEN, AND SOME YOU HAVE TO TAKE...
OPPORTUNITY? WHAT OPPORTUNITY?? YOU DITCHED US!
JIGGLE! JIGGLE!
WAAA-AA-AA!
KNOCK! KNOCK!
SCRATCH! SCRATCH!
MOMMY? MOMMY? MOMMY?

EWWW! YUK! WHAT'S SMEARED ALL OVER THIS ENVELOPE?

THAT'S NOT A SMEAR... IT'S A HORSE. ZOE PAINTED IT FOR YOU.

REALLY?
WOW! THAT'S INCREDIBLE!

IT'S AMAZING HOW SOMETHING CAN GO FROM DISGUSTING TO BRILLIANT WHEN YOUR CHILD IS INVOLVED.
KIRKMAN & SCOTT

WOW! YOU LOOK GREAT! WHAT'S THE OCCASION?
NO OCCASION... I JUST FELT LIKE GETTING A LITTLE DRESSED UP TODAY.

WELL! YOU SHOULD DO IT MORE OFTEN... ZOE! COME HERE AND SEE THIS!
KIRKMAN & SCOTT
SEE? PRETTY SKIRT... DANGLEY EARRINGS, NICE BLOUSE... ISN'T SHE PRETTY?
YEAH!

WHO IS DAT?

BIG BLAST WASH

NEW IMPROVED FORMULA! FIGHTS STAINS, DEFEATS DULL-NESS AND BRIGHTENS YOUR WASH BEYOND ALL REASONABLE EXPECTATIONS!
KIRKMAN & SCOTT

MY DETERGENT IS TRYING HARDER THAN I AM!

WELL, THE KIDS ARE IN BED... WHAT'S ON TV?
I'LL LOOK.

"FRIENDS," "PALS," "BUDDIES," "AMIGOS," "CHUMPS," OR "ACQUAINTANCES."

KIRKMAN & SCOTT

IS IT JUST ME, OR ARE ALL THE SHOWS ON TV STARTING TO LOOK THE SAME?
THEN THERE'S "SEINFELD," "SCHMINDFELD," "REINFELD"...

SO I GET THIS CALL TODAY...
BANG! BONG! BONG! BONG!
WHAT??

I SAID I GOT A CALL FROM...
BAM! BOM! BANG! BONG!
WHO? WHAT? WAIT A SECOND...

ZOE, MOMMY AND DADDY ARE TRYING TO TALK, WHY DON'T YOU WATCH TV FOR A FEW MINUTES?
GOOD IDEA.
O'TAY.

SO ANYWAY, I...
WHAT??
NO MONEY DOWN— NO CREDIT? NO PROBLEM! CALL—
KIRKMAN & SCOTT

The FATHER-DAUGHTER Relationship
HOW IT WORKS →

PLEEZ, DADDY? PLEEEEEZE??
WELL, OKAY...

PLEASE, ZOE? PLEEEEASE??
NO.
KIRKMAN & SCOTT

BABY BLUES®

BY RICK KIRKMAN / JERRY SCOTT

ISN'T THAT CUTE? HAM'S TRYING TO TALK TO US!
COO! GURGLE! GURBLE! OOOH!

GURGLE! SPOIT! BURGLE! BBBTH!
KIRKMAN & SCOTT

I THINK HE SOUNDS REALLY INTELLIGENT.
I THINK HE SOUNDS LIKE HE NEEDS A PLUMBER.
SLURP! GURGLE! GURGLE! POOEET! SPLIP!

...SO PIECE "A" FITS INTO SLOT "G" AFTER FLAP "R" GETS FOLDED UNDER THE— DON'T TOUCH DADDY'S TOOLS, ZOE!
ZOOMER PEDAL CAR
DIRECTIONS

THEN POST "D-1" POPS INTO THE HOLE ON DOOR PANEL "L", FORMING THE HINGE, WHICH THEN—HEY! NO! DADDY NEEDS THOSE SCREWS!
ZOOMER PEDAL

I CAN ONLY FIND TWO END CAPS! AND WHERE ARE THE LOCK NUTS FOR THAT— AAAGH! ZOE DON'T SWING THAT RATCHET!
BONK!

SO...HOW LONG DO YOU THINK IT'LL TAKE TO PUT TOGETHER?
BY MYSELF, ABOUT FIFTEEN MINUTES. WITH HER HELP, ABOUT A WEEK.
RIIPP!
KIRKMAN & SCOTT

WANDA, WHICH IS CORRECT: "I COULDN'T CARE LESS," OR "I COULD CARE LESS"?

"I **COULDN'T** CARE LESS" MAKES MORE SENSE, BUT MOST PEOPLE THESE DAYS SAY "I **COULD** CARE LESS." I THINK IT'S WRONG... WHAT DO YOU THINK?

I DON'T CARE!!

WELL, OKAY... FOR BREVITY'S SAKE, I GUESS THAT'S AN OPTION...
KIRKMAN & SCOTT

SIGH!
SIGH!

WHAT'S ON YOUR MIND?
DIAPER RASH, SORE NIPPLES, LAUNDRY, WOMEN'S RIGHTS, DISCIPLINE, THE NEW CHICKEN POX VACCINE, MY HAIR, HEALTH INSURANCE, POTTY TRAINING, —AND THE PRICE OF LETTUCE.

WHAT'S ON **YOUR** MIND?

PIE.
SIGH!
KIRKMAN & SCOTT

WHAT'S GOING ON?
ZOE FOUND AN OLD PACIFIER UNDER THE DRESSER AND SHE'S HAD IT IN HER MOUTH ALL DAY.

DO YOU THINK IT'S OKAY FOR NOW? DO YOU THINK IT'S BAD FOR HER TEETH? DO YOU THINK IT'LL BECOME A HABIT? DO YOU THINK WE SHOULD TAKE IT AWAY FROM HER?
I DON'T KNOW... WHAT DO YOU THINK?

WRAAAAAAAAAA!
POW!

I THINK IT'S OKAY FOR NOW.
WHAT A COINCIDENCE... THAT'S WHAT I THOUGHT, TOO.
KIRKMAN & SCOTT

WE'RE OUT OF MILK... WOULD YOU MIND RUNNING DOWN TO THE STORE?
SURE! I'LL TAKE HAMMIE WITH ME.

ALL RIGHT, BUT YOU'LL NEED A STROLLER, THE DIAPER BAG, HER TEDDY BEAR, A PACIFIER, A COUPLE OF DIAPERS, SOME POWDER, AN EXTRA SWEATSHIRT, A BLANKET, HIS JACKET, A HAT, MITTENS...

ENOUGH ALREADY! WE'RE JUST GOING DOWN TO THE CORNER FOR A GALLON OF MILK!
KIRKMAN & SCOTT

ADMIRAL BYRD DIDN'T NEED THIS MANY PROVISIONS TO GO TO ANTARCTICA!
ADMIRAL BYRD DIDN'T TAKE A TEN-WEEK-OLD BABY WITH HIM EITHER!

BABY BLUES®
BY RICK KIRKMAN / JERRY SCOTT

CRYPTIC... C-R-Y-P-T-I-C... CRYPTIC.

SSLURP!
MUNCH! MUNCH!

SO WANDA, DO WE HAVE ANY I-C-E--- C-R-E-A-M FOR D-E-S-S-E-R-T?

YES...BUT NOT UNTIL ZOE EATS HER P-E-A-S.

WHAT F-L-A-V-O-R IS IT? C-H-O-C-O-L-A-T-E?
KIRKMAN & SCOTT

NO...JUST V-A-N-I-L-L-A, BUT I B-O-U-G-H-T SOME C-H-O-C-O-L-A-T-E---S-Y-R-U-P AND LITTLE C-O-O-K-I-E-S TO PUT ON TOP.

THE C-O-O-K-I-E-S I LIKE WITH THE F-R-O-S-T-I-N-G ON TOP? Y-U-M!

WE DON'T HAVE MEALS ANYMORE... WE HAVE SPELLING BEES WITH FOOD.

BEFORE I HAD KIDS, I NEVER LOOKED AT WASHING THE UPPER HALF AND THE LOWER HALF OF A WINDOW AS TWO SEPARATE JOBS.

HEY, GARY!
HI, DARRYL.
MAIL

I JUST TALKED TO GARY.
REALLY?
KIRKMAN & SCOTT

WHAT'S NEW WITH THEM? DID GLENDA GET THAT STAIR-CLIMBER SHE WANTED? HOW DID HIS MOM'S FOOT SURGERY GO? DID HE SAY HOW THAT NEW CARPET CLEANER WORKED OUT? HOW WAS THEIR CAMPING TRIP? WAS IT FUN?
UH...

WELL?? YOU DID TALK TO HIM, DIDN'T YOU?
WELL... GUY TALK...

MOMMY? MOMMY? MOMMY? MOMMY?
MOMMY'S BUSY, ZOE!

WANDA? ARE WE OUT OF DIAPERS FOR HAM?
NO... THEY'RE ON THE SHELF IN THE LAUNDRY ROOM.

MOMMY? MOMMY?
WAAAAAAA!
CRASH!
WHERE? WHAT SHELF? I DON'T SEE THEM!
OKAY! OKAY! I'M COMING!

ONE OF THESE DAYS I JUST WANT TO BE ABLE TO STAY IN THE TUB LONG ENOUGH TO SHAVE BOTH LEGS...
KIRKMAN & SCOTT

WILL YOU BURP HAMMIE FOR ME, HONEY?
SURE.
SURE.

BETTER PUT A DIAPER BETWEEN HIM AND YOU... HE'S BEEN SPITTING UP A LOT LATELY.
OKEY-DOKEY!
OKEY-DOKEY!

PAT! PAT! PAT! PAT!
KIRKMAN & SCOTT

BABY BLUES®
BY
RICK KIRKMAN / JERRY SCOTT

WIPES

HERE, DADDY... IT'S YOUR TURN TO CHANGE HAM.
ME??

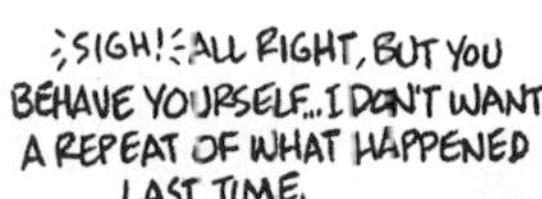
SIGH! ALL RIGHT, BUT YOU BEHAVE YOURSELF... I DON'T WANT A REPEAT OF WHAT HAPPENED LAST TIME.

OH YEAH! I FORGOT THAT HE WET ON YOU.
WET ON ME? HE DRENCHED ME!

I MENTIONED IT TO THE PEDIATRICIAN, AND HE SAID TO TRY WATCHING HAM'S TOES WHILE YOU'RE CHANGING HIM. SOMETIMES BABY BOYS CURL THEIR TOES RIGHT BEFORE THEY LET LOOSE.
REALLY?

WATCH HIS TOES, HUH? OKAY. I'LL TRY IT.

WATCH HIS TOES...
WATCH HIS TOES...
WATCH HIS TOES...

AAAAAAAGGGGHHH!!
KIRKMAN & SCOTT

DIDN'T WORK, HUH?
NO... AND WE'RE CHANGING PEDIATRICIANS.

TOOKEY!
THAT'S RIGHT...IT'S JUST A COUPLE OF DAYS AWAY.

TOOKEY! TOOKEY!

TOOKEY! TOOKEY! TOOKEY! TOOKEY! TOOKEY! TOOKEY! TOOKEY! TOOKEY!
KIRKMAN & SCOTT

TOOKEY! TOOKEY! TOOKEY! TOOKEY! TOOKEY! TOOKEY! TOOKEY! TOOKEY! TOOKEY! TOOKEY! TOOKEY!
I DIDN'T USED TO GET SICK OF TURKEY UNTIL A FEW DAYS AFTER THANKSGIVING.

SO, BRAD, BESIDES DATING MY SISTER, DO YOU HAVE ANY HOBBIES?
WELL, A FEW.

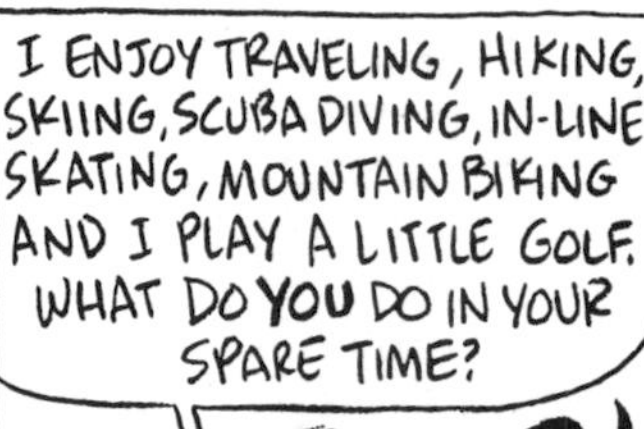
I ENJOY TRAVELING, HIKING, SKIING, SCUBA DIVING, IN-LINE SKATING, MOUNTAIN BIKING AND I PLAY A LITTLE GOLF. WHAT DO YOU DO IN YOUR SPARE TIME?

KIRKMAN & SCOTT

WA-HA-HA! HA! HA! HA!
HA! HA! HA! HA! HA!

WHAT DID I SAY?
"SPARE TIME." THEY ALWAYS LAUGH WHEN I SAY THAT, TOO.

SO YOU GUYS HAVE TWO KIDS, RIGHT?
YEP. ZOE IS TWO AND HAM IS THREE MONTHS OLD.

WOW! THAT MUST BE WEIRD.
WHAT? HAVING KIDS?

WELL, NO... NOT WEIRD TO HAVE KIDS. I JUST MEAN IT MUST BE WEIRD TO BE SO... SO...
SO PATIENT? SO MATURE? SO STRONG?

...SO WILLING.
KIRKMAN & SCOTT

TO DARRYL AND WANDA... IT'S A PLEASURE TO MEET PEOPLE WHO REALLY ENJOY BEING PARENTS.
HOW SWEET!

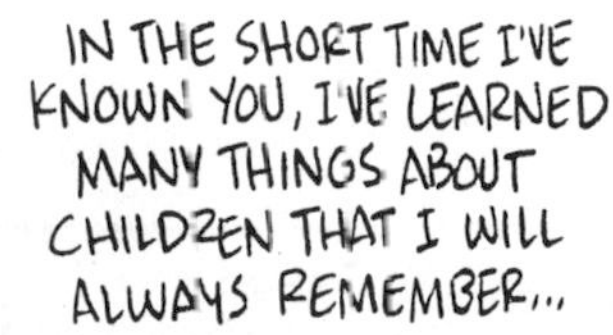
IN THE SHORT TIME I'VE KNOWN YOU, I'VE LEARNED MANY THINGS ABOUT CHILDREN THAT I WILL ALWAYS REMEMBER...

...LIKE, NEVER SIT NEXT TO ONE AT A MEAL WHEN GRAVY IS BEING SERVED.
AMEN.
KIRKMAN & SCOTT

YAAAY! WAHOOO! YES! YES! YES! WAY TO GO!!

WHAT HAPPENED?
ANOTHER TOUCHDOWN? INTERCEPTION? FUMBLE RECOVERY?
KIRKMAN & SCOTT

ZOE USED THE POTTY-CHAIR!!

AND YOU SAY THEY WERE NORMAL PEOPLE BEFORE THEY HAD KIDS?
SPOOKY, ISN'T IT?

CRUNCH!

#!!@%☆*!
DRAWER!!
☆#!!!

CUSSING DOESN'T HELP UNLESS YOU DO IT OUT LOUD.
WILDCATS UA
KIRKMAN & SCOTT

BABY BLUES®

BY RICK KIRKMAN / JERRY SCOTT

HMMM... THIS SAYS THAT ZOE SHOULD BE EATING 3-4 SERVINGS OF GRAINS PER DAY...

...PLUS 2-3 SERVINGS OF VEGETABLES, 2-3 SERVINGS OF FRUIT, ONE SERVING OF LEGUMES AND ONE SERVING OF MEAT, POULTRY OR FISH.

IT DOESN'T SAY ANYTHING ABOUT ART SUPPLIES.
I WONDER HOW MANY CRAYONS ARE IN A SERVING?
YOU & BABY
KIRKMAN & SCOTT

TELL ME THE TRUTH... IS HAVING TWO YOUNG KIDS TWICE AS MUCH WORK AS JUST ONE?
ABSOLUTELY NOT. NO. REALLY.

I EXPECTED IT TO BE TOTAL CHAOS AROUND HERE AFTER HAM WAS BORN, BUT IT ISN'T.
KIRKMAN & SCOTT

OH, SURE, WE'RE A LITTLE BUSIER AND THERE ARE MORE THINGS TO TAKE CARE OF, BUT ALL IN ALL, I THINK DARRYL AND I HAVE EVERYTHING UNDER CONTROL...

...DESPITE EVIDENCE TO THE CONTRARY.

YOLANDA, BUNNY AND I LOADED UP THE KIDS AND WENT TO THE FARMER'S MARKET TODAY.
WOW! ALL IN ONE CAR?

YEAH... FOUR CARSEATS, THREE TODDLERS, ONE INFANT, THREE WOMEN, PLUS DIAPER BAGS, STROLLERS, PURSES AND ASSORTED TOYS.

IT WAS A LOT OF WORK, BUT WE REALLY HAD FUN, AND THE VEGETABLES WERE BEAUTIFUL!

OF COURSE, THERE WASN'T ROOM TO BRING MUCH BACK...
KIRKMAN & SCOTT

...AND THAT'S HOW BUGGY BEAR GOT HIS NAME. THE END.
AGAIN?

NO, ZOE. NOT AGAIN. WE'VE ALREADY READ BUGGY BEAR **EIGHT TIMES IN A ROW** TONIGHT!
AGAIN!

NO! NO! NO! NO! NO! NO! NO! NO! NO! NO! NO! NO! NO! NO! NO! NO! NO! NO!

WHAT'S GOING ON IN HERE?
SHE'S BEING STUBBORN.
KIRKMAN & SCOTT

OKAY, ZOE... TIME TO WASH YOUR FACE, BRUSH YOUR TEETH, COMB YOUR HAIR AND GET DRESSED.
NOOO!

ALL RIGHT. YOU WIN. WE'LL COMB YOUR HAIR, WASH YOUR FACE, BRUSH YOUR TEETH AND **THEN** GET DRESSED.
OKAY.

WOW! YOU JUST LET HER THINK SHE'S IN CHARGE AND SHE GOES ALONG WITH WHATEVER YOU WANT HER TO DO... **VERY** IMPRESSIVE!
THANKS.

WHERE DID YOU LEARN THAT?
I'M MARRIED, REMEMBER?
KIRKMAN & SCOTT

WHAT DO YOU THINK OF MY SHADES, ZOE?
COO' MAN! COO'!

ISN'T THAT CUTE?
OH YEAH... REAL CUTE.
KIRKMAN & SCOTT

DARRYL, HOW CAN WE EXPECT HER TO SPEAK CORRECTLY IF YOU KEEP TEACHING HER SLANG?
OKAY! OKAY! DON'T GET SO EXCITED! IT'S NOT LIKE THAT'S ALL I TEACH HER, Y'KNOW.

CHIW OUT, BIG MAMA!
UH, WHY DON'T WE GO PLAY WITH YOUR PUZZLES OR SOMETHING?

BABY BLUES®

BY RICK KIRKMAN / JERRY SCOTT

WE'D BETTER START CHRISTMAS SHOPPING FOR THE KIDS PRETTY SOON.
ALREADY?

ALREADY??? ARE YOU KIDDING? MOST PEOPLE ARE FINISHED BY NOW!

IF WE WAIT ANY LONGER, ALL THE GOOD TOYS WILL BE GONE AND WE'LL BE STUCK WITH A BUNCH OF CHEAP, PLASTIC STUFF!
KIRKMAN & SCOTT

WE CAN'T AFFORD THE GOOD TOYS, SO DON'T WE END UP BUYING THE CHEAP PLASTIC STUFF ANYWAY?
DON'T GO CLOUDING THE ISSUE WITH LOGIC.

IT SEEMS LIKE ALL I EVER DO IS PICK UP TOYS AROUND HERE!

TOYS IN THE LIVING ROOM, TOYS IN THE BATHROOMS, TOYS IN THE HALLWAY, TOYS IN THE KITCHEN...

A PERSON CAN'T TAKE THREE STEPS AROUND HERE WITHOUT–

...TRIPPING OVER A TOY?
YEAH.
KIRKMAN & SCOTT

DARRYL, DO YOU EVER JUST LIE HERE IN BED AND THINK ABOUT THE FUTURE?
ME? OH YEAH! SURE!

LYING IN BED WAITING TO FALL ASLEEP IS WHEN I DO SOME OF MY MOST PROFOUND THINKING.

KIRKMAN & SCOTT

WHEN IT COMES TO THINKING, WOMEN ARE MARATHONERS AND MEN ARE SPRINTERS.
SNOFFCH!

OKAY, TOUGH GUY... PUT 'EM UP!
WHAT ARE YOU DOING?

BOXING WITH HAM.
WHY? BECAUSE HE'S A BOY? WHY DON'T YOU EVER BOX WITH ZOE?

IS IT BECAUSE SHE'S A GIRL?
NO.
BECAUSE IT'S NOT LADYLIKE?
NO.
BECAUSE IT'S A MAN'S SPORT?
NO.
THEN WHY?

SHE HITS BACK.
KIRKMAN & SCOTT

WASN'T ZOE ROLLING OVER BY HERSELF AT THIS AGE?
NO. SHE WAS FIVE MONTHS OLD... HE STILL HAS A FEW WEEKS TO GO.

WELL, DIDN'T ZOE HAVE HER FIRST TOOTH BY THIS AGE?
NO.
MORE HAIR?
NO.
BIGGER FEET?
NO.

KIRKMAN & SCOTT

BUT I DISTINCTLY REMEMBER BEING SOMEHOW AMAZED AT HER WHEN SHE WAS THIS AGE...
SHE WAS OUR FIRST BABY... WE WERE AMAZED WHEN SHE DROOLED.

OKAY, HAM-BOY, YOU AND I ARE GOING FOR A DRIVE.

WE HAVE TO GO TO THE HARDWARE STORE, THE LUMBER YARD AND THE TIRE SHOP.

JUST A COUPLE OF MANLY DUDES RUNNING SOME MANLY ERRANDS ON A SATURDAY MORNING.

AT LEAST AS MANLY AS TWO DUDES CAN GET WHEN ONE IS WEARING A BUNNY RABBIT SNOWSUIT AND THE OTHER IS CARRYING A FLOWERED DIAPER BAG.
KIRKMAN & SCOTT

BABY BLUES®

BY RICK KIRKMAN / JERRY SCOTT

WOOK, MOMMY!
CLOMP! CLOMP! CLOMP!

OH, YOU'RE WEARING BIG GIRL SHOES.

UNCOMFORTABLE, UNNATURAL, FOOT-PINCHING, CRIPPLING, AWKWARD, THROWBACK-TO-THE-STONE-AGE-OBJECTIFICATION-OF-WOMEN BIG GIRL SHOES!

BUT PERHAPS I'M TAKING THIS TOO SERIOUSLY...
MAYBE YOU SHOULD PLAY DRESS-UP WITH DADDY'S LOAFERS FOR NOW.
KIRKMAN & SCOTT

PEOPLE TALK ABOUT HOW HARD IT IS TO RAISE KIDS THESE DAYS, BUT I DON'T THINK IT'S ANY TOUGHER NOW THAN IT EVER WAS.

IT SEEMS TO ME THAT INVOLVEMENT AND CONSISTENCY ARE THE KEYS.

PARENTS WHO STAY INVOLVED AND ARE CONSISTENT WITH DISCIPLINE ARE LIKELY TO HAVE HAPPY, WELL-ADJUSTED KIDS WHO STAY OUT OF GANGS AND AWAY FROM DRUGS.
KIRKMAN & SCOTT

AT LEAST IT'S WORKING FOR US.
OF COURSE, IT HELPS THAT THEY'RE BOTH UNDER THREE YEARS OLD.

WE NEED A COMPUTER AT HOME FOR ZOE.
WHAT??

KIDS KNOW HOW USEFUL COMPUTERS ARE! KIDS KNOW HOW EDUCATIONAL COMPUTERS ARE! KIDS KNOW HOW MUCH **FUN** COMPUTERS ARE!

ZOE, DO YOU WANT A COMPUTER?
NO.
KIRKMAN & SCOTT

WHAT DOES **SHE** KNOW? SHE'S A **KID**!

ZOE, DO YOU WANT TO SIT IN YOUR HIGHCHAIR, OR IN A REGULAR CHAIR WITH A BOOSTER SEAT?
HIGH CHAIR.

OKAY THEN...
NO! BOOSTER SEET!

ALL RIGHT, I'LL JUST—
NO! HIGH CHAIR!
OKAY...
NO! BOOSTER SEET!
WHATEVER YOU S—
NO! HIGH CHAIR!
KIRKMAN & SCOTT

NO! BOOSTER SEET! NO! HIGH CHAIR! NO! BOOSTER SEET!
TODDLERS... GIVE 'EM AN INCH AND THEY'LL TAKE YOUR SMILE.

WEH! WEH! WEH!
UH-OH... THAT SOUNDS LIKE THE I-HAD-A-BAD-DREAM WHINE.

WEH! WEH! WEH!
OR MAYBE NOT. MAYBE IT'S THE I-DON'T-CARE-WHAT-TIME-IT-IS; I'M-HUNGRY WHINE.
KIRKMAN & SCOTT

WHUMP!

WEH! WEH! WEH!
NOPE. IT WAS THE YOU-MAKE-THE-COFFEE-AND-FEED-THE-KIDS-BREAKFAST-BECAUSE-I'M-TOO-TIRED WHINE.

##@☆!! CHEAP DISPOSABLE DIAPERS!
WHAT'S WRONG?

I JUST CHANGED HAMMIE AND THE STICKY TABS ON HIS DIAPER WOULDN'T STICK!
AGAIN?
KIRKMAN & SCOTT

YEAH! LUCKY FOR ME I ANTICIPATED THE PROBLEM AND WAS PREPARED.

THAT WOULD EXPLAIN THE DUCT TAPE.
IF YOU CHANGE HIM NEXT, YOU'LL NEED THESE.

BABY BLUES®

BY RICK KIRKMAN / JERRY SCOTT

DARRYL! COME QUICK! HAMMIE IS TRYING TO ROLL OVER!
REALLY?

THAT'S IT, HAMMIE! YOU CAN DO IT! (UNNH!) JUST A LITTLE (OOF!) MORE!
GO! TWIST! (OOMPH!) PUSH! (AGH!)

YES! HE DID IT!! ALL RIGHT, HAM! YAYY! WOOO-WOOOOO!
FLIP!
KIRKMAN & SCOTT

WHEW! THE OLDER I GET, THE TOUGHER THE MILESTONE.
YEAH... I DON'T KNOW IF I HAVE THE STAMINA TO WATCH HIM LEARN TO SIT UP!

THANKS FOR BABY-SITTING TONIGHT, RHONDA.
YEAH. IT'S THE ONLY WAY WE'RE EVER GOING TO GET OUR CHRISTMAS SHOPPING DONE.

LET'S GO... WE HAVE A LOT OF GROUND TO COVER.
KIRKMAN & SCOTT

WE HAVE TO GO TO THE MALL, DISCOUNT TOY SHACK, KIDS' OUTLET, COMPUTER GALAXY...

SO WHEN DO YOU THINK YOU'LL BE BACK?
HOW DOES A WEEK FROM THURSDAY SOUND?
...SHOEWARE-HOUSE, SOCKS ETC., EVERY-THING PLASTIC, THE WHISTLING MONKEY COWBOY BAND STORE...

DO YOU THINK ZOE WOULD LIKE THIS?
SURE, BUT LOOK AT ALL OF THE OTHER STUFF YOU HAVE TO BUY, TOO!
DOLLS
BITSY MITZI

THE CLOTHES... THE JEWELRY... THE HOUSE... THE CAR...
JEWELRY
MITZI PARTY DR.
MITZI'S CONDO
MITZI'S 'VETTE

IT'S SO SNEAKY. THEY CHARGE YOU A REASONABLE PRICE FOR THE DOLL, THEN THEY SOAK YOU FOR ALL THE ACCESSORIES!

SO YOU'RE SAYING "NO"?
I'M SAYING I DON'T WANT ZOE OWNING A DOLL WHOSE SHOES COST MORE THAN MINE.
KIRKMAN & SCOTT

OKAY. NOW WE NEED TO FIND SOMETHING FOR HAMMIE...
OH WOW! ELECTRIC FOOTBALL!

SEE? THE FIELD VIBRATES REALLY FAST AND THE LITTLE PLAYERS MOVE ALL OVER THE PLACE UNTIL THE ONE WITH THE BALL CROSSES THE GOAL LINE! THIS IS PERFECT! WHAT DO YOU SAY?
FOOTBALL FRENZY

DON'T BE SILLY... THE BOX SAYS IT'S FOR AGES SIX AND UP.
FOOTBALL FRENZY

WELL I'M SIX AND UP!!
HOTSHOT HOCKEY
BASKETBALL BATTLE
KIRKMAN & SCOTT

LOOK... HERE'S THE GIRLS' TOY SECTION. TELL ME WHAT YOU SEE.
A LOT OF PINK FRILLY STUFF.
GIRLS

RIGHT... AND HERE'S THE BOYS' SECTION... WHAT DO YOU SEE?
MACHINERY, THINGS WITH WHEELS, AND LOTS OF WEAPONS.
LI'L UZI
LI'L UZI

CORRECT. NOW WHAT DO YOU THINK THAT MEANS?
KIRKMAN & SCOTT

THE BOYS' SECTION IS MORE FUN?
NO! STEREOTYPES, YOU KNUCKLEHEAD! SEXIST STEREOTYPES!

WE'RE HOME!
FINALLY...
HOW WAS THE SHOPPING TRIP?
TOY SHACK

MADDENING! THE NOISE, THE CONFUSION... THE PUSHING & SHOVING...

...WE'RE TOTALLY WIPED OUT! HOW WAS THE BABY-SITTING?
KIRKMAN & SCOTT

YOUR EXPERIENCE, MULTIPLIED BY TEN.
SO THEY WERE GOOD, THEN?

BABY BLUES®
BY RICK KIRKMAN / JERRY SCOTT

HAM
ZOE
HO HO YOUR SELF

'TWAS THE NIGHT BEFORE CHRISTMAS, WHEN ALL THROUGH THE HOUSE NOT A CREATURE WAS STIRRING, NOT EVEN A M—
BOO-BOO BANKIE?
A Visit from St.

HERE'S YOUR BOO-BOO BANKIE, ZOE. NOW LISTEN WHILE DADDY READS US A STORY. START OVER, DADDY.
BOO-BOO BANKIE!

'TWAS THE NIGHT BEFORE CHRISTMAS, WHEN ALL THROUGH THE HOUSE NOT A CR—
WAAAAAA!
A Visit from

IT'S OKAY... HAMMIE IS JUST HUNGRY... START OVER, DADDY.

'TWAS THE NIGHT BEFORE CHR—
UH-OH... I THINK SOMEBODY NEEDS A NEW DIAPER!
PEEE-YEEWW!
A Visit from

KIRKMAN & SCOTT

OKAY, WE'RE BACK... START OVER, DADDY.
'TWAS THE NIGHT BEFORE CHRISTMAS... REINDEER ON THE ROOF... SANTA... PRESENTS... NOSE LIKE A CHERRY, BOWL FULL OF JELLY... "HAPPY CHRISTMAS TO ALL AND TO ALL A GOOD NIGHT!" THE END! LET'S ALL GO TO BED!
FLIP! FLIP! FLIP!
A Visit from

I TAKE IT THOSE AREN'T EXACTLY VISIONS OF SUGAR PLUMS DANCING IN YOUR HEAD...
@# !!!

NUTS! I THINK THERE'S SOMETHING WRONG WITH THE VIDEO CAMERA!

IT'S WEIRD... ALL I SEE IS A BLUR IN THE VIEW-FINDER. I WONDER IF—
UH, DARRYL?
WHAP! WHAP!

IT'S NOT THE CAMERA.
OH.
KIRKMAN & SCOTT

LOOK AT ALL THIS WRAPPING PAPER! I DIDN'T THINK WE BOUGHT THAT MANY THINGS THIS YEAR.

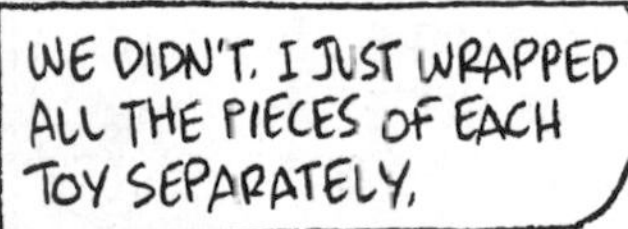
WE DIDN'T. I JUST WRAPPED ALL THE PIECES OF EACH TOY SEPARATELY.

THAT WAY, ZOE GOT TO OPEN LOTS OF PACKAGES, AND WE SAVED A TON OF MONEY ON TOYS!
THAT'S BRILLIANT! THAT'S INGENIOUS!

OF COURSE, WE ENDED UP SPENDING EVERYTHING WE SAVED ON ALL THE EXTRA WRAPPING PAPER.
...THAT'S TYPICAL.
KIRKMAN & SCOTT

WHERE ARE THE KIDS?
IN BED.

ALREADY? WOW! AND IT'S NOT EVEN EIGHT O'CLOCK!

WE HAVE THE WHOLE EVENING AHEAD OF US! AN ENTIRE NIGHT ALL TO OURSELVES!

SO WHAT DO YOU WANT TO DO?
Z
KIRKMAN & SCOTT

MONSTERS, DADDY! SCAWY MONSTERS!

IT WAS JUST A DREAM, SWEETHEART. THERE AREN'T ANY MONSTERS. THERE ARE NO SUCH THINGS AS MONSTERS.
SNIF! SNIF!
KIRKMAN & SCOTT

WEALLY?
REALLY.

Z

WHAT'S THAT SPOT ON ZOE'S SHIRT?
GRAPE JUICE.

NO, NOT THAT ONE... THAT ONE.
OH. PEANUT BUTTER, I GUESS.
KIRKMAN & SCOTT

NO, NOT THE PEANUT BUTTER... THE OTHER ONE. OVER... OVER... RIGHT THERE.
OH. THIS ONE?

THAT'S A CLEAN SPOT.
OH... NO WONDER IT LOOKED WEIRD.

I SAW DEMI MOORE ON TV LAST NIGHT AND SHE LOOKS FANTASTIC!
MPFG?

SHE'S HAD THREE KIDS, BUT SHE STILL HAS THE BODY OF A TWENTY-YEAR-OLD.
UMRG.
KIRKMAN & SCOTT

SHE'S JUST INCREDIBLE! AMAZING! A REAL INSPIRATION!

YOU HATE HER GUTS, THOUGH... RIGHT?
I HATE MORE THAN THAT, BUT DON'T GET ME STARTED.

BABY BLUES®

BY RICK KIRKMAN / JERRY SCOTT

TELL MOM "HAPPY NEW YEAR!"
APPY YOO NEER!

NO... "HAPPY NEW YEAR!"
APPY NOO NEER!

HAPPY NEW YEAR! HAPPY NEW YEAR! HAPPY NEW YEAR! HAPPY NEW YEAR! HAPPY NEW YEAR! HAPPY NEW YEAR!

THANK YOU, SWEETIE.
WAT HE SAID.
KIRKMAN & SCOTT

NO-NO, ZOE! YOU MUSTN'T TRY TO CARRY HAMMIE BY YOURSELF!
WHY?

BECAUSE. HE'S TOO HEAVY, AND IF YOU ACCIDENTALLY DROPPED HIM, HE COULD BE HURT!

OHHHHH...

NOW PROMISE ME THAT YOU WON'T TRY TO PICK HAMMIE UP AND CARRY HIM ANYMORE.
I PWOMISE.

WELL, I'M GLAD WE GOT THAT STRAIGHTENED OUT...
KIRKMAN & SCOTT

BLPH! BLPH! BLPH!
HA! HA! HA! HA!
GIGGLE! GIGGLE!

HAR! HAR! HAR! HAR! HAR!
GOO-PAH! GOO-PAH!
HEE! HEE! HEE!

KIRKMAN & SCOTT
HEH!
HEH!

BLAD-A-LADA LADA-LADA LADA-LADA LADA-LADA!
HEE! HEE! HEE! HEE! HEE! HEE!

HELLO?
MR. MacPHERSON? I'M CONDUCTING A VERY IMPORTANT SURVEY... COULD YOU TAKE A COUPLE OF MINUTES TO ANSWER A FEW QUESTIONS?

WELL, I... UH...UM...

HEY, ZOE — IT'S BEDTIME.

WAAAAA!
SORRY. I CAN'T HEAR YOU... YOU'LL HAVE TO CALL BACK.
KIRKMAN & SCOTT

SOMETHING WONDERFUL HAPPENED TODAY!
REALLY? WHAT?

IT WAS SO UNEXPECTED! I MEAN, IT HASN'T HAPPENED TO ME FOR A COUPLE OF YEARS!

IT TOOK ME COMPLETELY BY SURPRISE. I WAS MINDING MY OWN BUSINESS, TAKING CARE OF THE KIDS, AND BAMMO! IT JUST HAPPENED!
WHAT? COME ON! TELL ME!

I HAD A COMPLETE THOUGHT.
KIRKMAN & SCOTT

ARE YOU BUYING THAT BRAND?
YEAH- WHY?

THIS STUFF IS BETTER. IT HAS ENCAPSULATED SKIN SOFTENING EMOLLIENTS WITH NO ARTIFICIAL DYES OR PERFUMES
YEAH, BUT MINE HAS THE ACTIVE INGREDIENT HZ-412 AND A CREAMY WHITE CONSISTENCY.
KIRKMAN & SCOTT

DIRECTORY

GUY TALK JUST HASN'T BEEN THE SAME SINCE THEY TOOK CARBURETORS OUT OF CARS.
AMEN TO THAT.

BABY BLUES®

BY RICK KIRKMAN / JERRY SCOTT

WHICH DO YOU WANT TO DO...
A) CLEAN UP THE KITCHEN, OR
B) GET THE KIDS READY FOR BED?

KIRKMAN & SCOTT

WHAT HAPPENED TO C) NONE OF THE ABOVE?
IT WAS REPLACED BY D) IN YOUR DREAMS.

IT'S SO NICE TO HEAR FROM YOU, DEAR. HOW IS ZOE?
OH, FINE... SHE'S GREAT.

HOW'S THE POTTY TRAINING GOING?
VERY WELL.
KIRKMAN & SCOTT

WHENEVER SHE TELLS US SHE HAS TO GO, WE DROP WHATEVER WE'RE DOING, RUSH HER TO THE BATHROOM AND SHOWER HER WITH ATTENTION FOR AS LONG AS IT TAKES.

I'D SAY SHE HAS US COMPLETELY TRAINED.
SURE SOUNDS LIKE IT.

YOU KNOW, IT'S REALLY KIND OF GROSS TO BATHE THE BABY IN THE SAME SINK THAT WE USE TO WASH DISHES...
WHY?

GERMS! THINK OF THE BACTERIA THAT GET LEFT BEHIND IN THERE!
OH...

I GUESS THERE'S ONLY ONE THING TO DO.
YEAH.

STERILIZE THE SINK.
START USING PAPER PLATES.
KIRKMAN & SCOTT

ZOE MET A LITTLE BOY AT THE PARK TODAY.
BOY?

HE'S ALMOST EXACTLY A YEAR OLDER THAN SHE IS, AND HE'S REALLY CUTE.
AN OLDER BOY?

ZOE TRIED TO KISS HIM... AND SHE WASN'T THE ONLY ONE! HIS MOM SAID LITTLE GIRLS JUST LOVE HIM WHEREVER HE GOES.
AN OLDER BOY WITH EXPERIENCE!?

SO ANYWAY, I WAS THINKING OF INVITING HIM AND HIS PARENTS OVER FOR DINNER SOMETIME.
OVER MY DEAD BODY!!!
KIRKMAN & SCOTT

I CAN'T BELIEVE YOU'RE BEING SO SILLY ABOUT ZOE'S NEW FRIEND.

SILLY? KEEPING AN OLDER MAN AWAY FROM MY INNOCENT LITTLE DAUGHTER IS BEING SILLY??
WHAT OLDER MAN? HE'S THREE YEARS OLD!

OH SURE, HE'S ONLY THREE NOW, BUT SOMEDAY HE'LL BE FOUR, AND THEN FIVE AND THEN WHAT? HUH? THEN WHAT??
KIRKMAN & SCOTT

HE'LL BE SIX.
AH-HA!! SO YOU SEE MY POINT THEN!

SO I TOLD DARRYL THAT ZOE HAS FALLEN IN LOVE WITH A LITTLE BOY WHO IS A YEAR OLDER THAN SHE IS, AND HE WENT NUTS!

A GROWN MAN JEALOUS OF A THREE-YEAR-OLD BOY!
HEE! HEE!
USS KITTY HAWK CV 63

HAVE YOU EVER HEARD OF ANYTHING SO RIDICULOUS, MIKE?
HA! HA! NO...

...JUST TELL THE KID TO KEEP AWAY FROM MY KEESHA, OKAY?
KIRKMAN & SCOTT

BABY BLUES®

RICK KIRKMAN / BY / JERRY SCOTT

DARRYL MacPHERSON...
MAY I HELP YOU?

NO, WANDA... I CAN'T HERE. NO. PLEASE. DON'T...

HI, SWEETIE! YOU WENT TINKLE ALL BY YOURSELF? WHAT A BIG GIRL! YAYYYY ZOE! LET ME TALK TO MOMMY.
CLAP! CLAP! CLAP!
KIRKMAN & SCOTT

FROM NOW ON, LET'S SAVE THE POTTY-TRAINING REINFORCEMENT UNTIL I GET HOME, OKAY?

YOU'RE COLD, AREN'T YOU?
HOW DID YOU KNOW?
KIRKMAN & SCOTT

...TWENTY-(URF!) THREE...
...TWENTY-(UNNH!) FOUR...

FORGET IT. THIS IS JUST A WASTE OF TIME.

I'VE BEEN DOING SIT-UPS FOR WEEKS NOW AND IT HASN'T MADE A BIT OF DIFFERENCE.

WHAT'S THE BEST WAY TO GET A REALLY HARD STOMACH IN A SHORT PERIOD OF TIME?
GET PREGNANT.
KIRKMAN & SCOTT

WHOA! LOOK AT THAT GRIP! I'M THINKING QUARTERBACK, OR POWER FORWARD, OR PITCHER...
JUST BECAUSE HAM IS A BOY DOESN'T MEAN HE'S AUTOMATICALLY GOING TO BE AN ATHLETE!

WELL, OF COURSE... I DIDN'T... WHAT DO YOU...

KIRKMAN & SCOTT

IT DOESN'T??

I'M AFRAID I MUST WARN YOU—WE DON'T HAVE A CHILDREN'S MENU, NO BOOTHS, NO SPAGHETTI OR CHICKEN FINGERS, NO CRACKERS, NO CRAYONS, NO PAPER NAPKINS, AND WE INSIST ON PUTTING LOTS OF LIGHTED CANDLES ON EVERY TABLE.
YOU FIENDS!
LET'S GO!
KIRKMAN & SCOTT
HOW NICE RESTAURANTS STAY NICE.

HEY, EVERYBODY! HAMMIE CAN SIT UP ALL BY HIMSELF!

SEE? ALL YOU HAVE TO DO IS PUT HIS LEGS OUT... PROP HIS HANDS IN FRONT OF HIM...

WACHOO!

...AND AVOID ANY SUDDEN BREEZES.
KIRKMAN & SCOTT

BABY BLUES®

BY RICK KIRKMAN / JERRY SCOTT

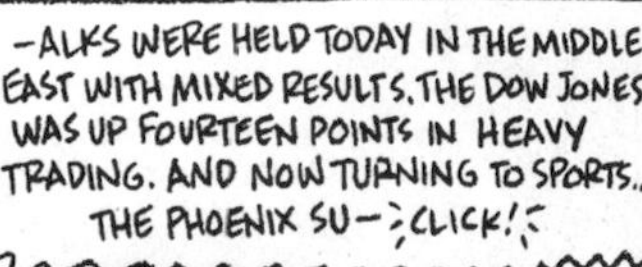

OH LOOK! A CARD FROM THE HAHNS!

IT'S A BIRTH ANNOUNCEMENT FOR LITTLE MACKENZIE!
AWWW... ISN'T THAT CUTE?

WAIT! THERE'S SOMETHING ELSE IN HERE...
WHAT IS IT?

LITTLE MACKENZIE'S FIRST-GRADE CLASS PICTURE.
I'M GLAD WE'RE NOT THE ONLY ONES WHO HAVE TROUBLE GETTING ANNOUNCEMENTS OUT ON TIME.
KIRKMAN & SCOTT

ARE YOU AWAKE?
SORT OF... WHAT'S WRONG?

NOTHING. I JUST KIND OF FEEL LIKE TALKING. IS THAT OKAY WITH YOU?
SURE.

SO LET'S TALK.
AGAIN?
KIRKMAN & SCOTT

THERE YOU GO, SWEETIE.

UPSIE-DAISY!

OKAY... OOF!.... WE'RE ALL SET!

THE TROUBLE WITH GOING TO THE GROCERY STORE THESE DAYS IS THAT MY CART GETS FULL BEFORE I EVEN START SHOPPING.
KIRKMAN & SCOTT

OKAY, ZOE... IF YOU GO POTTY IN THE POTTY CHAIR, YOU'LL GET A SPECIAL **STICKER** ON THE CHART!
A **STICKERRRR**! WOW! WON'T **THAT** BE SPECIAL!

NO GOOD. MAYBE BRIBERY ISN'T THE RIGHT METHOD.

MAKE THAT A STICKER **AND** THREE M&M'S.

THE METHOD WAS RIGHT... THE STAKES WERE TOO LOW.
KIRKMAN & SCOTT

BUNNY, YOLANDA AND I WERE THINKING ABOUT STARTING A BABY-SITTING CO-OP, BUT WE CHANGED OUR MINDS.

THE IDEA WAS THAT EVERY MONDAY, WEDNESDAY AND FRIDAY ONE OF US WOULD HAVE TO BABY-SIT ALL FOUR KIDS FOR FIVE OR SIX HOURS.

IT WAS A GOOD PLAN, EXCEPT FOR ONE MAJOR DRAWBACK.
WHAT DRAW-BACK?

EVERY MONDAY, WEDNESDAY AND FRIDAY ONE OF US WOULD HAVE TO BABY-SIT ALL FOUR KIDS FOR FIVE OR SIX HOURS.
KIRKMAN & SCOTT

I READ THAT PLAYGROUNDS AT PLACES LIKE THIS ARE JUST CRAWLING WITH GERMS.
YEAH. BUT IT KEEPS THE KIDS BUSY SO THE PARENTS CAN EAT.

THE FOOD IS LOADED WITH FAT, SALT AND SUGAR.
MMMMM... TASTES GOOD!

AND THESE FAST-FOOD CORPOR-ATIONS ONLY OFFER PART-TIME MINIMUM-WAGE JOBS WITH NO BENEFITS!
SO WE CAN AFFORD TO COME HERE MORE OFTEN.

GOODBYE CONSCIENCE, HELLO CONVENIENCE.
PLUS... **ACTION** FIGURES!
KIRKMAN & SCOTT

BABY BLUES®

RICK KIRKMAN / BY / JERRY SCOTT

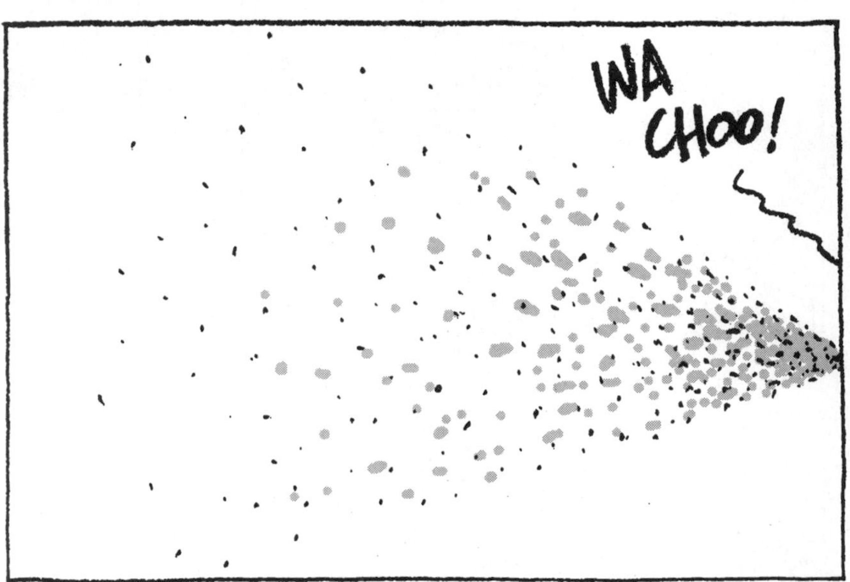

YOU KNOW HOW SCIENTISTS SAY THAT THE HUMAN BODY IS SOMETHING LIKE 86 PERCENT WATER?
YEAH...

WELL, THEY ALWAYS STOP THERE. THEY NEVER SAY WHAT THE OTHER 14 PERCENT IS!

BUT THROUGH KEEN OBSERVATION, I'VE FIGURED IT OUT.
OKAY. WHAT IS IT?
KIRKMAN & SCOTT

86 PERCENT WATER... 14 PERCENT MACARONI AND CHEESE.
SOMETIMES IT FEELS LIKE MORE THAN THAT.

I GO TO BED NOW.

HUH??
DID YOU SAY YOU WANT TO GO TO BED? VOLUNTARILY?
UH-HUH.

KIRKMAN & SCOTT

WELL, OKAY...
CAREFUL. IT COULD BE A TRAP.

WHEEEE! RIDE'EM COWGIRL!
WHEEE!

HEE! HEE! SNORT! SNORT!
WHEEE!
OKAY, THAT'S ENOUGH ROUGH-HOUSING... TIME FOR BED.

COME ON, ZOE.
KIRKMAN & SCOTT

YOU COULD GET UP AND HELP ME...
WANNA BET?

I DON'T THINK YOU SHOULD DO THAT.
WHEEEE!

OH YEAH? GIVE ME ONE GOOD REASON WHY NOT.

BECAUSE HE'S SCARED? HA! HE LOVES IT! BECAUSE HE'S TOO YOUNG? HA! I USED TO DO THIS TO ZOE WHEN SHE WAS YOUNGER THAN THIS!

HOW ABOUT BECAUSE HE JUST ATE.
OH-KAY... THERE'S ONE REASON...
KIRKMAN & SCOTT

YEAH?? WELL I DON'T CARE IF YOUR EQUIPMENT SAYS THE SIGNAL IS FINE... THE PICTURE IS COVERED WITH LITTLE BLURRY SPOTS!

YOU KNOW WHAT THE PROBLEM IS? I'LL TELL YOU WHAT THE PROBLEM IS! IT'S—
PEANUT BUTTER FUDGE BROWNIE FINGERPRINTS.

KIRKMAN & SCOTT

NEVER MIND.

OKAY ZOE... DON'T BE AFRAID. DADDY'S GOING TO BE WITH YOU ALL THE WAY DOWN, JUST LIKE ALWAYS. READY?
WEDDY.

WHEEEEEE!
WEE.

WOW! WHAT A RIDE! WASN'T THAT FUN??
KIRKMAN & SCOTT

SHE JUST DOESN'T SEEM TO GET AS EXCITED ABOUT THE PLAYGROUND AS SHE USED TO...
IMAGINE THAT.
YAWN!

BABY BLUES®

RICK KIRKMAN / JERRY SCOTT

I WANT YOU GUYS TO PLAY QUIETLY WHILE MOMMY EXERCISES, OKAY, ZOE?

HEY! DON'T TOUCH THE– GIVE ME THAT REMOTE! COME BACK H— WHAT'S WRONG, SWEETIE?
READY? BEGIN!
KIRKMAN & SCOTT

ZOE, IF YOU DON'T– SHHH! IT'S OKAY, HAMMIE. —I'M GOING TO COUNT TO THR– WHAT'S WRONG? ARE YOU HUNGRY **AGAIN**? HEY! NOT ON THE COUCH!
...AND FOUR! AND ONE, AND TWO, AND THREE–

...FEEL THE BURN?
OH YEAH...

ABSOLUTELY NOT!
WHY NOT??

IT'S FINE WITH ME IF YOU WANT TO GIVE HAM A NICKNAME. JUST NOT **THAT** ONE!
BUT WHY NOT?

DAVE IS "THE DAVESTER," MIKE IS "THE MIKESTER," BOB IS "THE BOBSTER..."

KIRKMAN & SCOTT

YOU ARE NOT GOING TO CALL **MY** SON "THE HAMSTER"!
OH WELL, BACK TO THE DRAWING BOARD...

RABBIT...
FLOWER...
BALL...
CLOUD...

CAR.
BLPR BLBBBBB!

AAAAGH!

WHAT??
TESTOSTERONE!
BBBBRRT! BBBBRRT!
KIRKMAN & SCOTT

COME ON, WANDA... JUST BECAUSE HAM LIKES THE PICTURE OF THE CAR DOESN'T MEAN HE'S GOING TO TURN INTO SOME TESTOSTERONE-SOAKED CRETIN.
BBBTHHTP!

SURE, HE'S A BOY. BUT BOYS ARE INTERESTED IN OTHER THINGS BESIDES CARS... WATCH!
PTHHBBBBB!

TREE...
DANCER...
WHALE...

...BAZOOKA...
AAAAGH!
UNH! UNH! UNH!
KIRKMAN & SCOTT

MOMMEEEWANNOOOEOO...
WOW! HAS ZOE BEEN WHINING LIKE THIS ALL DAY?

NOOOIIIWNANNGOOM...
I SUPPOSE YOU'VE TRIED EVERYTHING YOU CAN THINK OF TO GET HER TO STOP, RIGHT?

IIIMEEENOOOMAAA...
THERE MUST BE SOMETHING WE CAN DO...

I SEE THE BABY BOOK WASN'T MUCH HELP...
KIRKMAN & SCOTT

DO YOU THINK I'M GETTING A LITTLE HIRSUTE?
NO WAY.

REALLY?
HIRSUTE? YOU? DON'T MAKE ME LAUGH! YOU'RE A LOT OF THINGS, BUT HIRSUTE IS NOT ONE OF THEM!

THANKS, HONEY. THAT MAKES ME FEEL SO MUCH BETTER. SMOOCH!
KIRKMAN & SCOTT

HIRSUTE... HIRSUTE... H-I-R-...

BABY BLUES®

RICK KIRKMAN / BY / JERRY SCOTT

SHHH! BE QUIET, ZOE.
WHY?

HAMMIE IS ASLEEP, SO WE CAN'T MAKE ANY NOISE.
WHY?
BECAUSE WE MIGHT WAKE HIM UP.
WHY?
BECAUSE LOUD NOISES WAKE PEOPLE UP!
WHY?

BECAUSE THEY DO! THAT'S WHY!

WAAAA! WAAAAA!
SHHH! DADDY! HAMMIE WAS ASWEEP!
KIRKMAN & SCOTT

DING! DONG!
OH, GREAT! IT'S BUNNY!

MRS. PERFECT AT THE DOOR, AND WE'RE STILL IN OUR PAJAMAS!

WHAT AM I GOING TO DO? HOW AM I GOING TO EXPLAIN THE WAY WE LOOK?
DING! DONG!

TRICK OR TREAT?
KIRKMAN & SCOTT

COME ON, ZOE. LET'S MAKE A NICE VALENTINE FOR MOMMY.
O-TAY!

I THINK SHE WOULD LIKE SOMETHING WITH LACE AND HEARTS AND RIBBONS ALL OVER IT, DON'T YOU?
YETZ!

RIP!
TEAR
SQUIRT
SPLAT!
SPLAT!

HAPPY VALENTINE'S DAY.
KIRKMAN & SCOTT

WHERE'S MOMMY?

WHERE'S MOMMY? WHERE'S MOMMY? WHERE'S MOMMY?

PEEK-A-B—
WAAA-AAAA!

SIGH!
KIRKMAN & SCOTT

NO!
DON'T TELL ME NO... I'M YOUR MOTHER!

NO!
YES!
NO!
YES!

THAT DOES IT... DARRYL!
KIRKMAN & SCOTT

WHAT?
QUICK! DISAGREE WITH ME ABOUT SOMETHING... I NEED TO WIN AN ARGUMENT FOR A CHANGE.

OKAY! ALL THE BILLS ARE PAID AND I EVEN PUT A LITTLE MONEY IN THE KIDS' COLLEGE FUNDS!
REALLY? LET ME SEE.

THAT'S IT? THAT'S ALL YOU WERE ABLE TO PUT IN?

I CAN FIND THAT MUCH MONEY UNDER THE COUCH CUSHION!
KIRKMAN & SCOTT

WHERE DO YOU THINK I GOT IT?

BABY BLUES®

BY RICK KIRKMAN / JERRY SCOTT

IF WE'RE GOING TO A MOVIE THIS WEEKEND, WE'D BETTER FIND A SITTER.
NOT LISA. LISA'S TOO YOUNG.

HOW ABOUT ROCHELLE?
ROCHELLE CAN'T HANDLE TWO KIDS.
MADISON?
TOO WILD.
JENNY?
TOO SPACEY.

I'M SORRY! I HAPPEN TO HAVE EXTREMELY HIGH STANDARDS FOR BABY-SITTERS!
FINE.
KIRKMAN & SCOTT

THEN YOU CAN STAY HOME WITH THE KIDS WHILE I GO TO THE MOVIE.
WAIT! GO OVER THAT LIST AGAIN... I THINK I JUST FELT MY STANDARDS CLICK DOWN A NOTCH OR SO.

WHATER YOU DOIN'?
I'M FEEDING HAMMIE HIS DINNER.

BABIES DRINK MILK FROM THEIR MOMMIES' BREASTS, REMEMBER?
YUK!

EWWW! ICK! GWOSS!
KIRKMAN & SCOTT

THIS FROM SOMEONE WHOSE FAVORITE TOPIC OF CONVERSATION IS POOP.

AFTER A LONG DAY IN THE TRENCHES, THERE'S NOTHING I WOULD RATHER DO THAN SPEND A QUIET EVENING WITH MY FAMILY.

WAAAA!
OW!
PUT THAT DOWN!
CRASH!
WAAAA!
SPLAT!
KIRKMAN & SCOTT

A-A-A-AND SOMEDAY MAYBE IT'LL HAPPEN...

DON'T YOU HATE IT WHEN PEOPLE DON'T CONTROL THEIR OWN KIDS?
OH YEAH!

IT'S INEXCUSABLE! LOOK AT THAT ONE... TOTALLY OUT OF CONTROL!
YOU'RE RIGHT.

PUSHING OTHER KIDS OFF THE SLIDE... NOT TAKING TURNS... GRABBING TOYS... WHAT WOULD YOU DO IF SHE WERE YOURS?

DENY IT.
HI, MOMMY!
KIRKMAN & SCOTT

NO, ZOE. YOU CAN'T HAVE A COOKIE NOW.
PWEEZE?
WELL, OKAY.
KIRKMAN & SCOTT

NO, ZOE. YOU CAN'T GO OUTSIDE NOW.
PWEEZE?
WELL, OKAY.

NO, ZOE. YOU MAY NOT HAVE ANY SPINACH OR CAULIFLOWER.
PWEEZE?
WELL, OKAY.

PRETTY SNEAKY, HUH?
FOR A WHILE THERE YOU HAD ME WORRIED.
MUNCH MUNCH MUNCH

OKAY, MOM... I'LL TALK TO YOU LATER. TELL DADDY I SAID "HI."

HOW'S YOUR DAD DOING?
GREAT!

SINCE HIS HEART ATTACK, MOM SAID ALL HE DOES IS BRAG ABOUT HOW HE'S LOST 20 POUNDS, STOPPED DRINKING, WALKS THREE MILES A DAY AND WORKS OUT AT THE HEALTH CLUB.
WOW... I DIDN'T THINK HE COULD DO IT.

YOU DIDN'T THINK HE COULD GET IN SUCH GOOD SHAPE?
NO, I DIDN'T THINK HE COULD GET ANY MORE OBNOXIOUS.
KIRKMAN & SCOTT